WHAT PEOPL

WALKING *with the* SHEPHERD

"Angela Forker's experiences with the Italian shepherd are heartwarming and delightful. These stories are guaranteed to inspire your soul!"

—Denise Hunter
Bestselling author of the *Riverbend Romance* series

"In our modern day, the experience of a real shepherd is often lost or misunderstood. Angela's book 'Walking with the Shepherd' brings the depth of Scripture into reality and practically relates the journey of a shepherd and his sheep to each of our lives. Each story will bring you closer to the Great Shepherd's heart."

—Sarah A. Careins
Author of *Dream Beyond Yourself: A Journey
to Know God and Make God Known*

"Angela Forker's *Walking with the Shepherd* is a collection of modern-day parables showing us our need for the Good Shepherd. As you read each story, my prayer is that you will be inspired to be more, dream more, and do more of what God has called each of us to do."

—Minister Carol Copeland
Author of *I Am a Wife: Today's Wisdom for Single Women
that Your Mother and Grandma Didn't Tell You About*

Cover design by Sara Young
Cover Photo by Charity Slone

ISBN: 978-1-960678-69-0   1 2 3 4 5 6 7 8 9 10

Printed in the United States of America

WALKING

with the

SHEPHERD

INSPIRATIONAL STORIES FROM THE PASTURE

ANGELA FORKER

KUDU PUBLISHING

In memory of Antonio Spaltro, my special shepherd friend who lived in the small town of Castel D'Azzano by Verona.

We had so many meaningful talks and experiences out in the pastures surrounding our home.
I will never forget the lessons I learned while walking with the shepherd.

CONTENTS

Foreword..*ix*

Acknowledgments...*xi*

INTRODUCTION Walking with the Shepherd 13

CHAPTER 1. Understanding the Shepherd's Voice 17

CHAPTER 2. Blessings and Curses...........................21

CHAPTER 3. He Hears, He Sees, He Understands........ 25

CHAPTER 4. Carrying the Lambs in Our Arms 29

CHAPTER 5. That Still, Small Voice 35

CHAPTER 6. When He Says, "No".......................41

CHAPTER 7. The Making of a Staff 45

CHAPTER 8. Following the Crowd 49

CHAPTER 9. Hide and Seek 53

CHAPTER 10. Walking by Faith...................... 57

CHAPTER 11. Answering the Shepherd's Call 63

CHAPTER 12. Stale Leftovers........................ 67

CHAPTER 13. Ginger and Bo........................71

CHAPTER 14. Behold! The Lamb of God! 79

CHAPTER 15. I Just Want to Be a Sheep............... 83

CHAPTER 16. The Shepherdess....................... 87

CHAPTER 17. Where Is He? 93

CHAPTER 18. Mercy Mixed with Fear. 99

CHAPTER 19. The Shepherd's Touch 107

CHAPTER 20. He's Never Coming Back! 111

CHAPTER 21. Up Against a Wall. 115

CHAPTER 22. The Adoption 119

CHAPTER 23. Walking Uprightly 123

CHAPTER 24. You Can Make It! 127

CHAPTER 25. Walking with the Shepherd Again. 131

CHAPTER 26. Close to the Shepherd's Heart. 137

CHAPTER 27. Imperfect . . . but Forgiven! 141

CHAPTER 28. The Stray Lamb 145

CHAPTER 29. Feed My Sheep. 149

CHAPTER 30. There Is an Enemy!. 153

CHAPTER 31. The Shepherd's Kiss 157

CHAPTER 32. Finish to the End! 161

CONCLUSION He Knows Your Name 165

About the Author. *169*

FOREWORD

One of the greatest privileges I have as the CEO of *Four Rivers Media* is helping ministry leaders of all shapes and sizes broadcast their message to the world. In all my years working intimately alongside many first-rate ministry leaders, I'm convinced that leaders cannot effect change if they aren't changing themselves and the way they think about ministry. Even ministry takes ingenuity. In all my conversations with Angela Forker, one thing is crystal clear—she understands that as God is an out-of-the-box thinker, so are we to color outside the lines for the service and discipleship of His people.

What's more is that Angela's advocacy of ministry as a creative undertaking is markedly illustrated in Walking with the Shepherd. In this book, Angela—a tremendously generous servant of God with a heart the size of the entire state of Texas—demonstrates the humility and faithfulness of Christ to lower your position, get your hands dirty, and allow even the most unassuming of characters to enter your life so that you may impact others' lives. And this is exactly what she did. With zeal, she befriended the most unassuming character—a real-life shepherd.

What I admire most about Angela is her contrite heart to learn from those whom you may have otherwise assumed were too ordinary or too hidden to be used by God. This is the life-giving truth that abounds throughout the heartwarming stories of this book. Shepherds aren't lauded. They don't take center stage. Yet God used Angela's shepherd friend to demonstrate Christ's love for His sheep. As I read the stories about Angela's growing relationship with the shepherd, I noticed myself thinking, what kind of ripple effect did this have? As it turns out, this time with the shepherd was, in fact, another one of God's glorious displays of His innovation.

I was delighted to have the opportunity to learn from Angela about how God used her as a conduit to reach His lost sheep through the shepherd. With contagious enthusiasm, she said, "I have prayed over more unchurched people in my short time as a photographer than I did during our fifteen years as missionaries!" Angela's conclusions about the heart of ministry perfectly aligned with mine: ministry is more than just acts of service that occur within the four walls of a church. It is an invitation to open our hearts and minds to think big with God and accept that He is not traditional. In fact, He is unusually unorthodox in His methods to reach those who are far from Him. Angela takes this truth to heart. She walks the walk, and this is what makes her approach to ministry so unique and refreshing—just like God's.

Angela has inspired me to break out of the mold of traditional ministry paradigms and embrace God's call to do His work in the most ordinary places through the most ordinary people.

—Martijn van Tilbourgh
CEO of Four Rivers Media, Co-Founder of AVAIL

ACKNOWLEDGMENTS

Special thanks to my wonderful husband, Rick Forker, for putting up with all of my shenanigans. I know...I'm always up to *something*, and you're so patient with me. Whether I'm going out in a field to befriend an elderly shepherd, or taking *so much time* just to get the right photo, or writing a book of my many adventures, I can always count on your love and support. I love you, Hubby!

I am grateful for our daughters, Candace Brodhagen, Charity Slone, and Christina Balla. I will forever cherish the memories we made together with the shepherd, as you came out with me to visit him or helped me bottle-feed and care for his little lambs. We had so much fun together!

It is important that I thank my husband, Rick, and daughter, Charity, for taking the photos of me that are in this book. The photos I took myself only told part of the story. Because of the photos you took of the shepherd and me, my photos are able to be included in this book. Thank you, Charity, for going out into the field with me one evening to take some truly beautiful photos of the shepherd and me together. Your photos are some of my favorites. I'm so happy that we were able to incorporate them in this book!

The Kudu publishing team deserves my gratitude. For over a decade I have been holding onto these stories, knowing they were supposed to be made into a book. I had no idea how to make that book happen. Thank you for helping to make this dream a reality!

Most of all, I thank God, my Good Shepherd, for putting it in my heart to go out into the field and befriend a lonely, elderly shepherd. I would have never dreamed that I would learn so many lessons from one friendship...and that those lessons would turn into a book!

INTRODUCTION
WALKING
WITH THE SHEPHERD

"Hey, guys!" shouted one of our daughters as she looked out the window. "There's a shepherd outside! And he's surrounded by sheep and goats!"

My husband, Rick, and I, along with our three daughters, Candace, Charity, and Christina, were missionaries to Italy. We had just moved to the little town of Castel D'Azzano, just outside of Verona. We found a beautiful home that was surrounded by fields. On a clear day, you could see a gorgeous view of the Italian Alps . . . but my favorite part was the shepherd and his flock!

I scurried to the window, expecting to see a middle-aged man with a cape or something, with a long staff in his hands. I was surprised to see a very ordinary elderly man (he was then in his eighties) with a suit coat and a baseball cap. He held in his hand a very small staff that resembled a cane.

I watched him for months as he passed by our home with his flock. I was curious to know what it would be like to be a modern-day shepherd. I was kind of fascinated by it, too! We learned that in Italy, shepherds are allowed to bring their flocks to any field that isn't currently being used for a crop. He spent hours outside with his flock every single day, leading his flock from one field to another.

One day, I went out to see the sheep. I thought I might be able to pet some of them. I had no idea what trouble I would cause the shepherd when I tried to approach his sheep and they all scattered!

Later, I actually mustered up enough courage to go and talk to the shepherd. He seemed kind of mean to me. I was a little afraid of him at first, but he also seemed lonely. So, I kept going to visit him.

I could tell that he wondered why this crazy American woman would go out into the fields to talk to him and get close to his sheep. Besides that, he came from southern Italy and spoke a very different

Italian dialect. In the first few years, I usually had to ask him to repeat himself several times before I could understand what he was saying. But the more time I spent with him, the more I was able to understand him.

When he asked me what my husband did for a living, I told him he was a pastor. The funny thing is, the word for pastor in Italian is the same word for shepherd: "pastore". So, when I told him my husband was a pastor, he understood he was a shepherd! He got very excited and asked how many sheep he had! I played along a bit, but let him know our sheep were actually people and that my husband's flock was a beautiful group of international people in the church. We had a good laugh over that.

After a couple of years of faithfully visiting him, I won his friendship.

I'll never forget when I asked him, "Does it bother you when I come out to see you?"

He answered, "No, not at all. I actually look forward to your visits now!"

After time, I found him to be a very sweet, gentle friend. He was a faithful friend. I knew that since he went out to take care of his sheep each day, he would always be there.

Besides that, I got the blessings of fresh goat cheese, fresh ricotta, and hard cheese.

I treasured that friendship. But not everyone understood my friendship with the shepherd. The neighbors would watch as I'd run out into the field to visit the shepherd. I'm sure they were thinking, "What is she doing going out in the fields? Is she crazy?"

One of my good Italian friends said, "I've never heard of anyone going out into a field and befriending a shepherd."

You see, shepherds aren't highly esteemed. Ever since Bible days, they have always been regarded as second-class citizens. Part of the reason is that sheep have a very strong odor and that odor stays on your clothing and on your hands. It's part of being a shepherd! But I didn't mind having a friend who smelled like sheep. He loved his sheep. They were his life!

It didn't matter to me what others thought about my friendship with the shepherd. It was one of the most unique and special friendships I have ever had.

The stories in this book actually took place between 2007 and 2014. The shepherd was eighty-four years old when I met him and when we left Italy, he was a very spry ninety-one years old! We went to visit him once after we had moved back to the US, but after that, I never heard anything else from him. I always wondered how many more years he graced this earth with his presence!

Looking back at when I first met my shepherd friend, I could have never imagined that he would become one of my best friends over the course of those seven years, that I would have many exciting encounters with him and his sheep, and that I would be writing a book about our many adventures.

I am so very pleased to be able to share with you this special collection of stories about the lessons that I learned while walking with the shepherd.

CHAPTER 1

UNDERSTANDING THE SHEPHERD'S VOICE

When I first met the shepherd, his sheep wouldn't come near me at all. You see, sheep are afraid of strangers and only follow the voice of their shepherd. I learned this one day when I went to visit the shepherd while he was in the pasture. He had the entire flock in a tight little group in the middle of a field. He was steadily leading them back to the sheep pen and wanted to be sure they would stay together. As I went across the field to meet with him, I noticed that a number of sheep were starting to scatter a bit. I went over to the side of the flock, cutting off the stray sheep, causing them to run away from me and go back to the rest of the flock.

While I was merrily doing my good deed, I noticed that the shepherd was calling out to me, but I didn't pay much attention to what he was trying to say. I couldn't really hear him and—to be honest—I didn't think it was all that important. As soon as all the sheep were back together, I started to make my way to the shepherd, cutting through the flock. The shepherd was calling out to me again, but I figured I'd be with him soon and he could tell me whatever he needed to tell me when I got to him. I saw that he started making hand gestures . . . and then bodily movements. He was definitely trying to communicate something to me, but I just didn't get it.

Well, it turns out he was trying to inform me to go all the way *around* the flock, rather than go through it. But I didn't understand anything he was trying to say. I hadn't spent much time with the shepherd or his sheep at that point in time, so I didn't realize that as I walked, the sheep—afraid of me—were scattering away from me on *both* sides. I was like Moses parting the Red Sea!

By the time I got to the shepherd, I could see the regrettable consequences of not listening to him and trying to do things my way. Instead of bringing the flock back together, I actually ended up *dividing* it. Even though I meant well, I ended up creating chaos! Because of my foolish mistake, I made a lot of extra work for the shepherd.

As we make our way through life, we, too, may have great intentions, but if we don't inquire of God—our Good Shepherd—first, we could create a disaster for ourselves and for others around us! That is why it is so important that we learn to hear the Good Shepherd's voice.

How do we do this? We do it by spending time with Him, in prayer and in His Word, and by waiting and being still in His presence. The more time we spend with Him, the more we get to know His voice and the more we will understand His heart. As we learn to hear His voice, we learn not to jump ahead of Him but to wait until we hear Him speak. Hearing and understanding His voice makes all the difference!

Trust in the LORD with all your heart and do not lean on your own understanding; in all your ways submit to Him, and He will make your paths straight. —Proverbs 3:5-6

CHAPTER 2

BLESSINGS AND CURSES

"Look at those goats," the shepherd said to me. "They're always moving around everywhere." We watched together as the goats wandered away from him and the flock.

"Why is that?" I asked.

His answer caught me by surprise. "The goats are cursed," he replied. "The sheep are blessed."

I was trying to follow him, but I was clearly missing something. Then he finished his thought, "Who was there at Jesus' birth? Was it a goat? No, it was a lamb."

I had to think about that one a bit. Yes, very often you see pictures of, and even sing songs about, sheep being there beside the manger keeping baby Jesus warm. Yes, that may have been how it was, but I tried to think about the actual facts. What does the Bible say about the presence or lack of sheep? Uh ... actually, it says nothing. How about goats? Once again, nothing is mentioned. That doesn't mean there were no sheep there. It's possible there were. But who's to say there weren't some goats there, too?

I had to chuckle at the shepherd's strong words. Maybe he was just having a bad day with the goats? The shepherd may or may not be right about the presence of sheep at Jesus' birth, but there is one thing he *does* know: that his sheep generally follow and obey him while the goats run away from him and constantly disobey him. I guess it's no wonder why, in my shepherd friend's opinion, the goats are cursed and the sheep are blessed.

That made me think of a couple passages in the Bible. The first one is in the book of Matthew, where Jesus said that when He comes to set up His kingdom, He will separate the sheep from the goats (Matthew 25:31-46). He will call the sheep blessed as He places them to His right. From there they will enter into His eternal presence. On the other hand, He will place the goats on His left side and will send them to eternal . . . well . . . anyway . . . He calls them cursed!

Hmmm . . . maybe my shepherd friend isn't the only one who thinks the goats are cursed!

The other Bible passage that comes to mind is in the book of Deuteronomy, where God offers His children blessings or curses (Deuteronomy 28). It is the great desire of our Good Shepherd to bless His children. He wants to shower blessings on every area of our lives! *But* His blessings are *always* followed by an "if"—they are conditional. We will be blessed *if*—like the sheep—we will follow our Good Shepherd with *all* our hearts and obey His Word. *If*, however, we choose to go our own way—like the goats—we will be cursed.

I can illustrate this concept well using the shepherd's sheep and goats. The goats constantly disobey him, going wherever they wish and doing whatever they please. Whatever he says to them, they do the opposite! They prefer to eat stale, unwholesome food and to be frequently exposed to danger. When difficulties arise, they face them alone. They are often in trouble. The goats intentionally *choose* to forego the blessings of walking closely to the shepherd. And what does the shepherd think about them? He calls them cursed.

However, he calls the sheep blessed! They listen for their shepherd's voice. When he speaks, they obey him! When he disciplines them, they receive his correction because they want to please him. They follow the shepherd closely as he gently leads them to the nutritious food that strengthens their bodies and to the refreshing water that satisfies their thirst. He keeps them safe in his presence; he helps them through their difficult moments; he heals them when they are sick; he saves them when they are in danger. The shepherd is pleased with their loyal obedience and blesses them with his constant protection, presence, and provision. His sheep find comfort, peace, and rest when they remain by his side.

That sounds just like my Good Shepherd! If I choose to follow Him with all my heart, listen for His voice, read His Word, and do what is right—letting go of the things in my life that are not pleasing to Him—those same blessings will overflow in every area of *my* life!

Blessings and curses. The choice is ours! Do things our own way, and we miss out on our Good Shepherd's blessings. But, if we do things *God's* way, we are blessed! I choose . . . blessings!

"When the Son of Man comes in his glory, and all the angels with him, he will sit on his glorious throne. All the nations will be gathered before him, and he will separate the people one from another as a shepherd separates the sheep from the goats. He will put the sheep on his right and the goats on his left. Then the King will say to those on his right, 'Come, you who are blessed by my Father; take your inheritance, the kingdom prepared for you since the creation of the world.'" —Matthew 25:31-34

CHAPTER 3

HE HEARS, HE SEES,
HE UNDERSTANDS

t's hard to decide what my favorite part of walking with the shepherd has been. I have loved seeing the sheep around our home, hearing their *baas*, watching the lambs jump and play, and learning about the sheep while talking to the shepherd. My favorite part, though, has probably been the times I've helped him with his sheep—especially little lambs.

On one occasion while I was in the field with my shepherd friend, he abruptly stopped talking. "Do you hear that?" he asked me.

I stopped to listen. All I could hear was the sound of many sheep bleating.

"There is a lamb that is in trouble," he said.

I listened again, but I couldn't hear anything out of the ordinary. How could he know that?

He inspected his flock and figured out which lamb was missing. He looked around as he listened intently.

Even though I couldn't hear it, I figured he must know what he was talking about. I looked around but couldn't see anything unusual. I looked into the neighboring fields. Still, I couldn't see anything.

Without delay the shepherd left the flock to search for his missing lamb, just as I had seen him do several times before. He was responding to a cry that I couldn't even hear. We went through a wooded section that divides two fields. When we did, he pointed to a faraway thicket and said, "There he is."

I couldn't hear him and I couldn't see him, but the shepherd had already spotted him and even understood his need.

The shepherd quickened his pace. As we got closer, I could finally hear the distressed lamb's cry for help. A little later I could see the thicket that ensnared the little lamb. When we reached him, I saw that he was pretty small. Somehow, his wool had gotten tangled inside a thorny thicket." He was growing weak from struggling and crying.

The shepherd quickly got his staff and started pulling back the thorny branches while I reached down and pulled the lamb out of the thicket. "Can I hold him?" I asked the shepherd. It isn't very often that I get to hold a lamb, so this was another special moment for me. I carried him back to the flock where he quickly ran back to his mama.

How wonderful for that little lamb that the shepherd heard his cry. If it had been up to me, he would have remained trapped and would have likely been attacked by a dog or some wild animal.

But I guess that is why he is the shepherd and not I. When I hear nothing, he hears the distant cry of a little lost lamb. When I see nothing, he sees a lamb that needs to be saved. When I don't understand, he already knows the need.

Oh, how this speaks to me of our Good Shepherd! When no one else hears you, Jesus hears your desperate cry for help. When no one else sees you, Jesus sees you right where you are. When no one else understands you, Jesus already knows your need. He hears you. He sees you. He understands you.

Won't you call out to Him today? If you do, He will come running to save you!

"... call on me in the day of trouble;
I will deliver you, and you will
honor me."—Psalm 50:15

CHAPTER 4

CARRYING THE LAMBS
IN OUR ARMS

t was a day much like any other. When I woke up, I could hear the faint bleating of sheep in the distance which meant that the shepherd was passing by our home with his flock of sheep.

That morning as I knelt to pray, God spoke to my heart. He said, "I want you to go out and seek the lost sheep." Immediately I thought about people I knew who had strayed away from Him. I thought about people who didn't know Him yet. I asked Him to show me how I might reach them for Him and how I might lead them to their Good Shepherd. Little did I know that shortly after my prayer time, I would have an experience that would become a real-life parable.

As the morning went on, the sound of bleating continued to fill the air. It was strange, though. I couldn't quite explain it, but something was different. First of all, it had been raining and the shepherd doesn't usually take the sheep out in the rain. Another thing is that the shepherd and his flock usually go from field to field and the bleating of sheep gradually fades in the distance. Strangely, I had been hearing this bleating for hours and instead of coming from different fields, it had been continuously coming from only one side of our house. Lastly, as I listened more carefully, I realized that it wasn't the normal occasional bleating that we would hear from the flock. No, as I focused on the sound, I could hear that it was the lonely, high-pitched cry of a little, lost lamb. (I later found out he was only three days old.) All kinds of thoughts filled my head: *Had he been out there all night in the rain? How long could such a young lamb make it without its mother? Would I be able to catch it?*

I quickly left the house and stood at the end of our dead-end street, scanning the field to catch sight of the lamb. Of all the neighbors that heard the bleating, only a couple tuned into the cries and knew that something was wrong. And there we were at the edge of the field, all of us searching for the little lost lamb. Wouldn't you know. . . . it was at the very far end of the field! And here's the thing: it was one thing to hear the cries; it was another thing to tune into them and know that something was wrong. But it was an entirely different thing to be the one to leap into the field and go and rescue that lamb. You see, the grass in the field was so tall and wet. If someone was willing to rescue that lamb, they were going to get wet . . . and dirty! Worst of all, if they caught the lamb, they were going to get stinky! (Sheep have a strong odor! If you are near them for a long time—especially if you hold one—that odor stays with you and just won't go away!)

Without thinking about how filthy I was about to become (or how much of a show I was going to give to my girls—and my neighbors), I jumped into the field.

As I approached the little lamb, he became terrified. He sprang to his feet and ran away as fast as he could. I could see that it was going to be difficult to catch him! I had to run to try to keep up with him. After a few minutes of chasing him all over that field, I started to think it was hopeless. Still, I kept following him and after a long, hard chase, the little guy was worn out and I was finally able to reach him.

I caught him in my arms. I was so excited! I shouted to my girls, "I caught a lamb!"

He didn't like it at first. His long legs stuck out of my arms stiffly. He cried and he cried as he struggled to get away. The poor thing didn't realize that I had come to *help save him*. I held him close and spoke soothing, gentle words to him. Finally, in the warmth of my arms, he could see that it was a good, safe place. Almost instantly his crying stopped and after a while, he lay in total surrender.

My girls came with a towel. He was so cold that he was shivering. We dried him off and cleaned him up a bit. We took turns holding him. The more we loved on him, the more he trusted us. He kept sniffing us and nuzzling his little nose into our necks, looking for something to eat. He was so hungry—he needed his mama! Luckily for that lamb, I knew the shepherd well. He was my friend! I had even been to his place on several occasions, so I knew the way to his home. The whole time we walked there, the girls and I were all so excited about saving a little, lost lamb!

After a long walk, we were at the shepherd's place, carrying the lamb in our arms. The shepherd was happy to have his lost lamb back. He took him and put him back in the pen and the little lamb excitedly ran to find his mama. Lambs have long tails. When they are happy, their little tails wiggle. How sweet it was to see his little tail wiggle for joy as he drank his mama's milk!

The little lamb was safely back with the shepherd. My job was finished.

As I was walking back home, God spoke to me. He said that my job was *not* finished, because all around me, there are lost sheep, crying out for help.

I guess if I think about it, though, this would apply to all of us! Our job is *not* done. All around us there are lost sheep that—one way or another—have wandered away from the safety of our Good Shepherd. We need to be sensitive to hear their cries. It may be hard to find them and even more difficult to reach them. At times it may be dirty, hard work. So often they will try to run away, but if we are persistent and speak to them with loving, kind words, they may sense our warmth and surrender to the wonderful love of our Good Shepherd, Jesus.

An important thought: if we are going to bring them back to Him, we ourselves need to know the Good Shepherd. Otherwise, how will we know how to help them find their way back home?

May Jesus find us doing what He Himself did: seeking and saving that which was lost. May He find us all carrying the lambs in our arms.

"For the Son of Man came to seek and to save the lost." —Luke 19:10

CHAPTER 5

THAT STILL, SMALL VOICE

"The sheep are *right* in front of our house!" called my daughter from her upstairs window. She and I went out to the porch with my husband to watch as the shepherd led his flock through the field in front of our house. It's so much fun watching each of the sheep jump over the ditch as they enter the next field.

My husband noticed a couple of sleeping lambs in the field. Christina and I went a little closer and saw that they were no more than a week old. The shepherd and the flock were getting farther and farther away, and we knew that the farther away they were from the shepherd, the harder it would be for us to get them back to him.

Our first job was to arouse them and show them that they needed to be close to the shepherd. Then we had to either catch them and bring them back to him or guide them to go in the right direction. This isn't as easy as you may think. I tried speaking to them to kind of coax them to go back to the shepherd. But there were several problems. First of all, they had no idea what I was trying to tell them. Besides that, the little lambs didn't know me. Even if they did, sheep only listen to the shepherd's voice. They also frighten very easily and they had no idea that we were there to help them! I ended up running around in circles trying to catch them and realized that that was not going to be an option. Then I found myself doing the same thing, just trying to get them to go the right way! It soon became obvious to me that we were going to have to strategize a bit in order to get these little guys going in the right direction!

I went on one side and Christina went on the other as we tried to direct them to cross the path and jump over the ditch, just as all of the other sheep had done. When we got them there, they didn't want to jump over it. I will admit that for such a little lamb, that ditch was a pretty big leap. It wasn't easy, but they finally jumped over the ditch. Christina and I jumped over the ditch and continued on with the chase. Now all we had to do was get them across this next field, which led to the field where the shepherd was with the rest of the flock.

As we guided the lambs across the field, I started to wonder how we were going to get them to cross over into the next one. It was then that the shepherd spotted us from afar and saw what we were doing. He motioned to us to steer the lambs to the side with the narrow path that led from our field to his. The plan seemed so easy, but those little lambs did not want to go in the right direction! They went this way and that, but they just wouldn't go to the side of the field where the narrow path was. I ran quickly to cut them off and finally got them to turn around. At last, they were headed in the right direction, but no matter what I did, I couldn't get them to go down that narrow path. I even tried catching them again, but it was hopeless. I just couldn't do it.

Just then, the shepherd did something I'd never seen him do before. He began to call out to them with an affectionate call. I was amazed at how these little lambs—only one week old—already knew the shepherd's voice. Even though it was so distant, they knew it was his voice. Immediately, they stopped and looked up. He called out, and they answered with a little cry. He called out again and they eagerly responded. They continued this way while Christina and I guided them in the right direction. Now, they *willfully* crossed the narrow path and made it into the shepherd's field. He continued calling out to them and they simply followed his voice, crying out in joy the whole way across the field until they reached him.

By the time Christina and I got to the shepherd, the lambs had already found their mother. Both of their little tails wagged excitedly as they drank their mother's milk. The shepherd laughed with us at the beautiful sight.

There is so much about this story that speaks about how we should go out and find the lost sheep and how Jesus, our Good Shepherd, helps us as we lead them on the narrow path that brings them to Him. But what I want to focus on today is hearing the voice of the Shepherd.

Just as the shepherd called to the flock when it was time to follow him to the next field, Jesus is calling out to each one of us, "Come! Follow me!" And the interesting thing is, his sheep know his voice! But some of us are like those little lambs that were sleeping and didn't hear his voice, and maybe some of us are like the lambs that were so busy playing that they were distracted and couldn't hear him when he spoke.

It is so important for us to know that Jesus, our Good Shepherd, loves His sheep so much. All He wants is for us to come to Him. And while He uses the people around us to bring us to His side, one of the most compelling things He does is to call out to us, "Come, my precious one. Here I am. This is the way. You can make it! Come, follow me."

Have you ever heard God's voice? He is calling out to each one of us. He has so much He wants to tell us! But if we want to hear Him, we must stop and listen.

Take some time today to be still in God's presence. Ask Him to speak to your heart.

When He does, it will be a still, small voice, a whisper in your soul . . . and if you can hear it, it is the most powerful force of all!

Whether you turn to the right or to the left, your ears will hear a voice behind you, saying, "This is the way; walk in it." —Isaiah 30:21

CHAPTER 6

WHEN HE SAYS, "NO"

One day while I was walking with the shepherd, I followed him as he led the flock into a new field. There was a situation that he needed to make his flock aware of. They could graze in this new field, but not in the field beside them—even though the sheep and goats had been eating in that other field all winter long. There was a new crop planted there now. Even though it would be more appealing to his flock, it was now forbidden.

With grunts, the shepherd made it clear that they were not to go into the neighboring field with the crop. The sheep understood and stayed right beside the shepherd. They were like, "Oh, the shepherd brought us to this field and he doesn't want us to go to that one. Okay."

The goats, however, didn't want to understand! Immediately, several went into the forbidden field. In response, the shepherd made his "Geh!" noise. The funny thing is, only the ones who were guilty lifted up their heads! They knew they were doing wrong!!! They lifted up their heads and went running out of that forbidden field—only to go back into it a few minutes later! I watched the shepherd make his noise at one goat after another. They just kept testing him, "Did you *really* mean we couldn't go into that field? Why not? We just ate there last month and it was fine!"

Some goats kept going into that forbidden field even after the shepherd said no. It was as though they were saying, "Hey dude, can't you see that that food would be better for us?" At that point, it was discipline time. The shepherd threw his staff at them and came after them. You didn't have to tell them which direction to go.... they knew! The one stubborn goat that kept disobeying even got a little whack when the shepherd got to him.

God really spoke to me again that day. How many times does He say, "No!" and we counter, "But why not?" Sometimes we try to reason. . . . "But, God, don't you see that this would be better for me?" or, "But it was okay before." God knows that maybe it would hurt us . . . or maybe it would hurt someone else. There are simply things God knows that we do not know. Like that field, it was okay last month, but now it is not. But in a few months . . . it will be okay again! It's just that the timing wasn't right.

The bottom line is: our Good Shepherd loves us. He knows what is best for us—and those around us. Many times, we just don't understand. We can't see the big picture, but God does! His ways are high above our ways. Our job is simply to follow our Good Shepherd, trust Him . . . and obey.

Just remember. If He says, "No" . . . obey Him! Or like those goats, discipline may follow!

"For My thoughts are not your thoughts, neither are your ways My ways," declares the LORD. "As the heavens are higher than the earth, so are My ways higher than your ways and My thoughts than your thoughts." —Isaiah 55:8-9

CHAPTER 7

THE MAKING OF A STAFF

One afternoon I came upon the shepherd while he was sitting on the edge of a little canal watching over his sheep. In his hand was a stick that was bent over and tied with a piece of wire. He had a knife which he used to whittle away the bark and little branches.

Bewildered, I asked him, "What are you making?"

"I'm making another staff," he answered, as he showed me the crack in his old staff. "My old one is broken."

I was shocked. There was no way that that ugly stick in his hands tied with a makeshift wire was ever going to look like a staff! "*That* is going to be a staff?" I asked him.

"Yes," he replied. "After I work on it a bit longer, it will look like my old one."

I looked at his old staff. I had seen him use it for years to guide the sheep, discipline the goats, and rescue little lambs. It was smooth and perfect—*nothing* like the crude branch he held in his hands. I was amazed, because I always thought he had bought it somewhere!

"You made that yourself?" I asked him. "But how did it get so perfect?"

"First, I had to find just the right kind of plant—one that I could bend easily," he replied. "Then I cut off a branch. Next, I made a little fire and heated it for about five minutes so I could bend it and make the curve. After that, I tied it just like this one," he said, as he lifted the stick and pointed to the curve. "I found this piece of wire nearby, so I used it to tie the stick," he continued. "Now I just need to cut away the bark and little branches until it is clean and smooth, free from the imperfections. After a while it will dry and look like my old staff."

I went back home and just couldn't stop thinking about the shepherd's staff. So smooth. So perfect. So greatly used by the shepherd.

At that moment God spoke to me. He showed me that we are like that shepherd's staff! You see, not all of us are called to be shepherds—or pastors—but Jesus, our Good Shepherd, wants to use *all* of us to help Him with His work!

At first, we are like that crude stick—a branch from a bush that most people would think would never be of any use! But Jesus, our Good Shepherd, sees what others cannot see. Instead of seeing a weed, He sees a valuable instrument! He looks for someone who is pliable. He takes us and allows us to go through the fire, though not for too long—and not to destroy us—but just long enough to be able to mold us into a usable form. Next, He uses the things around us to continue to shape us into that important tool—just like the wire the shepherd found in the field. Still, He hasn't finished yet. He needs to cut away our imperfections. With every whittle of the blade—with the Sword of the Word of God—He is cleansing us. No, it isn't a pretty sight at first, and at times the process can be quite painful, but if we will allow Him to do His expert work, He will make us into that beautiful staff—one that He can use to guide His sheep in the right direction, to rescue those who are in danger, and to correct those who are going astray.

I saw the shepherd again about a week after I had seen him making his new staff. I had been thinking about it all week long and I was surprised to see that he was still using his old one.

"How is your new staff?" I asked him. "It isn't ready yet?"

"No," he answered. "It's back at my house. I still have to wait for it to dry for about another week and then it will be ready to use."

I thought about that. I thought about it long and hard. I remembered a time in my life when I believed I was ready to be used by God, and instead, I felt like I had been placed on a shelf, forgotten by Him. I felt so alone. I even wondered if He still had plans to use me ... and if He had forgotten my name. But my Good Shepherd hadn't forgotten about me. He was thinking about me all the time. I was there, safe in His house. This time of waiting was necessary because even though on the outside I may have looked like a staff, on the inside, I wasn't yet strong enough to do the work He needed me to do. This time of waiting was a time of strengthening and maturity because not only does He need an instrument that He can use, He also needs it to be durable, able to withstand great difficulties, be dependable, and last for many years.

Sometimes waiting is the hardest part. God may seem so far away. But we need to remember that He is still making us. He has a plan. We need to wait for *His* timing. He knows when we will be ready. And then our Good Shepherd will take us into His hands once again—the beautiful staff that He, Himself, created—and He will use us to do *many great things* for Him!

For we are God's handiwork, created in Christ Jesus to do good works, which God prepared in advance for us to do. —Ephesians 2:10

CHAPTER 8
FOLLOWING THE CROWD

Walking outside, I could hear the familiar bleating of sheep. It's a sound I have grown to love over the years. On this one autumn day, however, it was a little bit different than usual. While most of the sheep were in the field to the left of our house, the bleating that filled my ears was coming from a different direction.

Before I knew it, about six sheep came running out of the field, crossing over the dirt road and darting into the next. They were running away from the shepherd and the rest of the flock and were following what seemed to be an errant ring leader.

Curious, I walked over to the shepherd. As I was walking to him, I noticed that half of the flock decided to chase after the wayward ones.

"Look at that troublemaker," the shepherd said angrily, "She ran off and led half of the flock astray!"

We both looked into the next two fields. In the closest field, we saw the majority of the rebellious sheep just running around aimlessly. In the field beyond it, we saw the five sheep running wildly behind their ring leader. They looked like little specks, just frolicking and running around in circles. They looked ridiculous!

I couldn't help but wonder how the shepherd was going to get his flock back together again. What work for him—all because of that one delinquent sheep.

Once again, the shepherd spoke. I was a little surprised by his words. He said, "Sheep are so dumb. If one jumps into the water, all the others will go and jump in the water and drown with it."

Just as he spoke those words, I saw how very much we are like sheep. How many times have we heard that sentence: "Everyone else is doing it!"? While this may seem true, it does not make it right. Very often what comes after that sentence is one who finds himself running wildly and frolicking in fields of sin. They forget about the consequences of sin—and most of all—that it separates us from Jesus, our Good Shepherd.

Such behavior saddens our Good Shepherd, so much so that He will leave the rest of His flock to go out and seek and save those who have gone astray.

There was something else that I saw in the shepherd that day. Although he was sad about those who had chosen to leave him and the rest of the flock, he was clearly angry at the one who had led them all astray. This is something very important to remember in life. It's one thing if we decide to go astray, but it's much more serious if we are responsible for leading others astray.

This makes me want to look at my life very carefully. I never want to be guilty of leading others astray. Instead, I want to lead them *to* the Good Shepherd! I want to be sure that I am following Jesus with all of my heart—no matter what anyone else does! I want to please my Good Shepherd.

In a world where everyone seems to be following the crowd, may He find us following Him with all our hearts!

Do not follow the crowd in doing wrong. —Exodus 23:2

CHAPTER 9
HIDE AND SEEK

"Two days ago, a little lamb was born," the shepherd told me. "It is so beautiful. You have to see it!" I was out in the field with my shepherd friend. I could tell he was very proud of his newest little lamb by the way he was describing it. "Come," he said with a twinkle in his eye, "I'll show it to you."

The shepherd looked all around him, but it was not there. He looked to one side of the flock, but he didn't see it. He looked to the other side, but it was simply nowhere to be found. At that moment a worried look came over his face. "It must have stayed in the other field," he said. Immediately he left all of his sheep and quickly made his way to find the little lost lamb. I followed him into the most recent field he had been in with his flock. We looked in the canal; we looked all around the field but simply couldn't find it. I noticed that now the shepherd looked very concerned. He didn't give up his search. He picked up his pace and walked all along the field.

At last, at the far end of the field, we found the tiny lamb sleeping behind a low bush. The shepherd took his staff and gently put the nook around its neck to get a hold of it. He took it in his arms and let me pet it.

I looked at the shepherd. He was smiling broadly. Yes, he was very proud . . . and so happy that his lost lamb had been found!

As these events were happening, I couldn't help but think about the parable that Jesus told about the man who left his ninety-nine sheep to find his lost lamb. When he found it, he greatly rejoiced!

But my story doesn't end here. When my shepherd friend placed the lamb back down on the ground, it still seemed kind of lost. The shepherd had to take his staff and guide it as it walked. Whenever it went the wrong way, the shepherd just used his staff to steer it until it went in the right direction.

Then we got to the dreaded ditch. "Look, it can't make it over the ditch," the shepherd said. He picked it up in his arms and carried it over to the ground on the other side. By the time we got back to the other field, most of the sheep had already gone on ahead. Once again, the young lamb was confused, but the shepherd didn't get angry with it. He patiently guided it with his staff until it was back with the rest of the flock and safely by his side.

I was very moved by the great love and patience the shepherd demonstrated to his newest little lamb. Not only did he leave all of his other sheep to find it, but he stayed by its side, continuing to direct it until he was sure it was headed in the right direction.

Do you know that you have a Good Shepherd who feels the same way about you? His name is Jesus. He doesn't want any of us to perish. He, too, is searching for His little lost lambs, and He rejoices when He finds us. But it doesn't end there. His love is *so great*! He stays by our side, gently guiding us in the right direction. If we get confused and start going the wrong way, He doesn't get angry. He patiently steers us and instructs us in the way we should go. He is ever by our side, even carrying us when we get discouraged or feel we can't make it on our own. *Oh, what love*!

If you are that little lost lamb, the Good Shepherd wants you to know that He loves you and that you are precious in His sight.

Maybe you feel discouraged or confused and you're not sure what direction you need to go in. Allow the Good Shepherd to find you and take you into His arms. Allow Him to direct you with His staff.

No matter where you are in life, if you will surrender everything to Him, He will come and save you. He promises to lead you and guide you and always be by your side!

"What do you think? If a man owns a hundred sheep, and one of them wanders away, will he not leave the ninety-nine on the hills and go to look for the one that wandered off? And if he finds it, truly I tell you, he is happier about that one sheep than about the ninety-nine that did not wander off." —Matthew 18:12-13

CHAPTER 10

WALKING BY FAITH

Walking with my shepherd friend isn't always easy. Sometimes I run out to meet him when he and his flock are directly in front of our home. That's easy. Other times I have to go out and really seek him before I can find him. This was the case one hot, dry summer afternoon.

I had heard the bleating of sheep a bit earlier but wasn't able to leave the house at that moment. At least I knew that he was somewhere nearby. I went outside and listened. Initially, I heard nothing, but after a while I could hear the whisper of bleating far in the distance. It was kind of strange, because when I looked out the shepherd was nowhere in sight. Nowhere in sight ... yet I knew he was out there. So, I set out in search of my shepherd friend like I had done so many times in the past.

I listened and tried to figure out where the bleating was coming from. As far as I could tell, it was coming from behind the left-most fields. I headed off in that direction. Even though I couldn't see any sign of him or his sheep, I was guided by the small sound of bleating that echoed through the fields. Since it echoed, I couldn't be sure that I was headed in the right direction, but still, I kept moving on. My persistence was rewarded when I saw that first sheep, and then another, and then I saw the whole flock of 150 sheep all crammed in this tiny little field that was all closed in by trees and bushes. I didn't even know there was a field back here! I smiled as I saw how green this field was. We had passed a very hot, dry week and the shepherd had found a nice green pasture for his sheep!

I didn't see the shepherd yet, so I called out, "Ciao! Ciao!"

The shepherd knows my voice, so of course he answered me, but at first it was hard for me to discern his voice.

I called out to him again. "Dove e'?" ("Where are you?") And then I just stopped and listened for His voice.

"Eccomi qua!" ("Here I am"), he yelled, as he appeared out of a thicket. "I'm making a new path for my sheep."

I had to laugh when I saw him. He was cutting away at all of those bushes with a little pocket knife and knocking them away with his staff. The shepherd was making a new path for his sheep so he could lead them to an even greener pasture that lay beside a spring of fresh water!

As he led the sheep through the new fields, the grass was so high that at times we couldn't even see the sheep! He kept making his guttural noise as we continued to press forward. The sheep simply followed him by staying together and listening for his voice.

At one point, one of the sheep found itself cut off from the rest of the flock, lost in the deep meadow. He cried out in panic. The shepherd heard his cry and answered with his own call. That sheep cried out again and ran towards the shepherd.

The shepherd and I both laughed. "He knows my voice," he said.

Even though that sheep wasn't able to see the shepherd, he was able to reach him *simply by listening for his voice.*

Next, we went through a small wooded area where the grass was even taller. At the end, the sheep were rewarded with a long drink of fresh water from a sparkling brook. What a pleasant treat for those sheep on this hot summer's day!

It made me think of the first two verses in Psalm 23: "The Lord is my shepherd, I lack nothing. He makes me lie down in green pastures, he leads me beside quiet waters, he refreshes my soul."

On the way back, we cut through yet another new field with grass higher than any of the other fields we had been in. The shepherd continued to call out while the sheep made a new path in the field. At one point, I was surprised that the shepherd left the sheep on their own in that overgrown field while he and I took the dirt path back.

Now, I will be honest with you here. This was a new field for those sheep. The grass was well above their heads. In that moment, I felt like he was abandoning his sheep at a time when they really needed him. I questioned him, "Don't they need you to help them make it through this tall, new field?"

"They'll find their way," he responded. "They'll make it out at the end of this field and at that tree, they will cross the road to the other field."

Was it true? Would they really do it just as the shepherd had said?

He watched over his flock as the sheep made their way through the high field, *baaing* at each other in order to stay together. I watched in amazement as the sheep made it to the end of the field. Then—instead of going ahead to the next field—they turned at the tree and crossed the road, going into the other field—*just as the shepherd had said!*

So the shepherd knew what he was doing all along! I was amazed to see that he knew his sheep so well. He knew what they were capable of. He *knew* they would make it!

From the beginning to the end of this tremendous shepherd encounter, God was speaking to my heart.

Maybe *you* are like those sheep out there in the field. The grass is over your head. You feel like you're in a maze. Worse yet . . . you feel like He has abandoned you. In moments like these, you need to trust and have faith that your Good Shepherd knows what He is doing. He knows you can handle this! He even knows the path you will take. He has *not* abandoned you. He loves you so much! He *knows* you are going to make it! Just keep following Him by faith, and it will all make sense in the end.

When I thought about the beginning of my adventure that day, as I set out to find my shepherd friend, it reminded me of when we seek God. Sometimes He's right there before us. We simply reach out and touch Him. Other times we really have to seek Him to find Him. We seek and seek His face and may even wonder if He's really there. In moments like that, we just have to have faith that He *is* there. And very often, if we will just stop and listen, we can hear that still, small voice in our hearts, giving us the evidence that He *is* near. After all, we have that promise that if we seek Him, we *will* find Him.

Once we have found Him, we need to follow Him, just like those sheep. Sometimes He brings a big change in our lives. Yes, change can be difficult, but it is also good. We learn to depend on Him and we learn that we can do a lot more than we thought. Through it all, He shows us His faithfulness. He brings us to still waters to refresh our souls. Other times our Good Shepherd may lead us through a complicated maze full of thickets, trees, and high grass. We may question, "What are you doing, God?" "Why are you letting this happen to me?" "Why aren't you here with me during my time of need?"

We can learn a thing or two from those sheep. During times of difficulty, we need to continue to put our faith in our Good Shepherd. We need to stay close to the flock (the family of God). We also need to listen for the voice of our Good Shepherd. If we do happen to lose our way, all we have to do is cry out and listen for His voice. Once again, we may not be able to see Him, but by faith, we know He is there. And if we listen, we will hear His voice, saying, "This is the way; walk in it."

It is often during some of the most difficult times of our lives that we learn to depend on our Good Shepherd. It is in those moments that we discover that He is always there—that He is *always* faithful!

As we walk with our Good Shepherd, we will learn to walk by faith and not by sight.

And without faith it is impossible to please God, because anyone who comes to him must believe that he exists and that he rewards those who earnestly seek him. —Hebrews 11:6

CHAPTER 11

ANSWERING THE SHEPHERD'S CALL

t was so peaceful in the field this beautiful spring evening. Every once in a while, I could hear the bleating of a little lamb. Most of the sheep were lying down. I love seeing the sheep rest because it means that the shepherd has done his job. He has led the sheep to fresh pastures throughout the day. They have eaten and are satisfied.

Now it was getting late. The sun would be setting soon and it was time for the shepherd to round up his flock and bring them back to the sheep pen. The shepherd called out to his sheep. They understood that he was telling them, "Come! Follow me!" It was time to go back to the pen for the night. Little by little they gathered around him. The shepherd knew that there were often some little lambs that were sleeping and hadn't heard his call, so he and I went around the field and woke them up. He nudged them with his staff while I said things like, "Svegliati! Segui il pastore!" ("Wake up! Follow the shepherd!") And then we led them in the right direction.

One little lamb was extra sleepy. She was newly born and didn't seem to be able to wake up and follow the flock. The shepherd roused her again and got her to join the rest of the sheep, but he knew she wasn't strong enough to keep up with them yet. He called my name and asked me if I would carry her back to the pen. I wasn't sure if she would let me pick her up, so I was very happy when she did! She was so tiny and frail . . . and so cute! Oh, how I love holding new little lambs! She came in close to me, grateful for the warmth of my body. I talked to her the whole time, telling her how sweet she was and that one day, she was going to be big and strong enough to keep up with the flock on her own. For today, though, the shepherd had asked me to come and carry her. . . . and I was happy that I was there to help!

I looked at the shepherd. He is kind of like a father to me and I am like a daughter to him. At that very moment, I could see a deep appreciation in his eyes—an appreciation because I had answered his call to help him. But more than that, an appreciation because I take time to be with him. Because I am his friend.

I can't express how much I enjoy spending time with my shepherd friend and how I love being there to help him. I have found that the more time I spend with him, the more his sheep trust me. The more time I spend with him, the more I am able to help him—and the more he asks me to help him! That is because I know his heart. I have even come to know some of his thoughts. I know his needs and desires. And he knows that my desire is to be there to help him.

It is very much the same way with our Good Shepherd. He is our Heavenly Father. He knows every one of us by name. He is calling out to each of us! He wants us to follow Him. To be His friend. He wants us to come and spend time with Him. To know Him. To know His thoughts. To know His heart.

He wants to use us!

How much would it please Him if we would just ask Him, "How can I help you, Jesus? What can I do for you?" Who knows. Maybe there is a little lamb around you that is too weak to make it on their own today. Maybe our Good Shepherd is calling out to you to take that one into your spiritual arms and carry them with your prayers and encouraging words until they, too, are able to walk tall and strong on their own with our Good Shepherd.

Can you hear the Shepherd's call? He is calling *you* by name. He's saying to you, "Come and follow Me!" "Be my friend!" "Spend some time in my presence!" "Come and help Me. I have need of you!"

If you will answer His call, you will see that He has *great* things in store for you!

Then I heard the voice of the Lord saying, "Whom shall I send? And who will go for us?" And I said, "Here am I. Send me!" —Isaiah 6:8

CHAPTER 12

STALE LEFTOVERS

This summer I've found myself with the shepherd almost every day that I've had some free time. It's been nice, because not only have I been getting closer to the shepherd, but since I've been spending so much time with him, even the sheep have been starting to get used to me. Initially, they were afraid of me, but one afternoon while we walked together I could see that something was changing. The shepherd was leading the sheep across a field he had just brought them into. As the sheep pushed forward to follow the shepherd, they crowded around me as though I wasn't even there. Even a little lamb came up to me and actually let me pet him. I was thrilled! In my earlier years with the shepherd, the sheep would do all they could to avoid me. By now they have come to learn that if the shepherd has confidence in me, they can, too. I love this trust that the sheep have for the shepherd. I would see it more in the events that were to follow that day.

I looked out at the flock. They seemed very peaceful as they grazed in the field. Little by little, some of the sheep were changing their direction and started drifting backward toward the sheep pen. I knew that the shepherd wasn't leading them that way, but it was such a minor change that I didn't think it would cause a problem. The shepherd, however, thought differently. He went toward the drifters and abruptly started making his deep grunting sound. It's always amazing to me that the sheep actually understand what he is trying to convey with his guttural grunts! They quickly turned back around and returned to him in the center of the field where he had led them before.

I personally didn't understand why the shepherd had made such a big deal of this. It didn't seem that unusual to me. In fact, it was quite common for the sheep to spread out a bit as they were grazing.

It's not as though they were running off. They were just going back a little bit to where they had come from. So why did he rebuke them so quickly and make them return to him?

The shepherd must have seen the questioning look on my face. He explained to me, "If I let them go there now, they'll keep going back in that direction (he pointed to the fields they had already come through that day) and they won't get enough to eat."

I was speechless. While I thought it was such a little thing, he knew it would turn into something big. He cares about his sheep. He wants to be sure they are going to get the nutrition they need. If he let them go backward, they would go where there was no longer any fresh food. The shepherd had a plan. He knew what was best for his sheep! And he wanted his sheep to follow *his* plan! The good news is that the sheep immediately accepted his correction. They decided to trust that their shepherd knew what he was talking about. They obeyed him by returning to him and not going back into the other field. In doing so, they were rewarded with fresh food rather than stale leftovers.

In much the same way, we may find ourselves going back to old habits or allowing things from our past to creep back into our hearts and lives. At first, we may not think anything of these trivial changes, but if we are sensitive to our Good Shepherd, we will hear Him speak to our hearts. It may be a voice of encouragement, warning, or even discipline. He does this because He loves us! Our Good Shepherd has a plan for our lives. He cares about each one of us. He wants to lead us into fresh, green pastures, where we will become spiritually fat! Still, too often we find ourselves drifting backward. Just a *little* bit, though, you know? Not doing any of the *really bad* things. And then we sense God's rebuke. We may wonder why He's making such a big deal of something so small. It's not like we've gone all the way back to our sinful lives! But He understands the consequences we may not be aware of. He knows that when we start drifting backward, we may in fact end up back where He's taken us from . . . or even worse! Even if we don't end up fully backsliding, we will be settling for stale leftovers instead of the rich, divine food He has for us. In doing so, we will never grow to the spiritual maturity He wants for us!

Jesus is calling out to us to come back to Him with all our hearts. When He admonishes us, we need to stop and evaluate. What is He saying? Why is He saying it? Have we allowed things to come into our hearts that could prevent us from being all He wants us to be—or even separate us from Him? If we have, we need to accept His correction, trust that He knows what is best, obey Him, turn away from these fleshly desires, and return to our Good Shepherd with all our hearts!

May we have this one determination every day of our lives: I am *not* going back to stale leftovers! I am going *forward* with Jesus to receive *all* that He has for me!

If you consent and obey, you will eat the best of the land. —Isaiah 1:19, NASB

CHAPTER 13

GINGER AND BO

"Hold the bottom of the bottle up high," the shepherd told Candace. My daughter lifted it up a bit higher. The little white lamb quickly guzzled down the goat's milk. We all laughed as his little tail wagged with joy. His brother came and tried to drink from the bottle, so Candace gave him a turn as well. Just as his brother had done, his little tail wagged in delight. What a lovely sight!

"I love the orange one so much," cried Charity. "He's so cute!" She held him in her arms and he licked her face.

"Let's call him Ginger," said Christina.

Everyone agreed it was the perfect name for him.

This summer we had a very special opportunity. The shepherd told us about twin lambs that were born prematurely. The mother was too sick to care for them, so they had to be bottle-fed. For a couple of weeks my girls and I would go out to the sheep pen to help the shepherd feed these adorable little preemies.

Normally these little lambs would have been out in the fields with the rest of the flock, but this month the flock was far away in a fenced-in area. We felt so bad that they were all by themselves, so one day we offered to take them to our home for a couple of days. Somehow, the shepherd agreed! People looked at us rather curiously as we walked back home, each of us with a tiny lamb in our arms.

At last, we made it back. "They're here!" squealed Christina. She and Candace ran out of the house to join us.

"Now we need to come up with a name for the white one!" said Christina. "I know, how about Bo, like on *Garfield and Friends*?" Yes, it was ideal. Now they each had a name: Ginger and Bo.

Just then, Bo came to me, let out a little cry, and pushed his head back and forth into my knee, just like the little lambs do to their mothers when they are nursing. "He thinks I'm his Momma!" I exclaimed. I reached out to touch him and he instinctively went to suck my finger, his long tail wagging crazily.

Little Bo's back end was covered in crusty filth. "The first thing these guys need is a bath!" I announced. So, we got an old dish basin, filled it with water, and brought it to our front porch.

I washed Ginger first. When he was all clean, Christina wrapped him in a towel and cuddled with him to warm him up.

After that, it was Bo's turn. Just as I was scrubbing his hind end, a delivery man came to deliver a package. He just stood there in bewilderment, as if waiting for an explanation. (I guess I hadn't really considered how ridiculous I looked, sitting on my front porch, scrubbing a lamb's bottom in a dish basin!)

I looked at him and said, "Sono senza parole." ("I am without words.")

Looking quite baffled, he answered, "Anch'io!" ("Me, too!")

With that, we both burst into laughter.

After a while, the little lambs were clean. Bo ended up being so soft and puffy! While they were still drying, they cuddled up to Christina and fell asleep on her.

Later that day, as Charity entered the house, I heard her exclaim, "Best—idea—*ever*!"

For two days, we had the pleasure of cuddling, feeding, and playing with these lovable babies. They followed us wherever we went! Ginger loved to be cuddled, while Bo was more independent. If we left them alone, however, Bo was the one who would cry—and cry like a baby! They even learned to climb up the stairs onto our porch. They would go to the screen door and cry until someone went out to be with them. As soon as one of us went out, they would run to us and suck our fingers, tails wagging excitedly.

On Friday it was time to take Ginger and Bo back to the shepherd. We remembered that he had given us some homework. He told us not to carry them back, but to have them follow us, in order to teach them to eventually follow the shepherd. That was pretty easy in our yard, but in the big open field, it ended up being much more challenging than we had thought! They got confused and distracted. Even when we called them, they simply didn't know where to go! Our typical fifteen-minute walk to the sheep pen took about an hour. By the end, though, those lambs were finally following Candace and Charity . . . well, *somewhat* anyway.

Back at the pen, we fed them their last bottle. "I think it's time for them to join the rest of flock," the shepherd announced. This was very sad for us, because we knew the sheep were still going to be away for another two weeks. We wondered if they would even remember us anymore. After saying goodbye, we sadly walked back home.

All we could think of was those darling little lambs. They were so weak and had depended fully on us in order to survive. We wondered if they would make it.

"We should have kept them," said Charity, "That way we'd be sure they'd be okay."

"They're not our lambs, Charity," I answered, "We had to bring them back to the shepherd and the other sheep where they belong. We've done our part, and now we just need to trust that they'll be okay."

A couple of weeks passed. Finally, the shepherd was back in the fields by our home with his flock. Looking out into the field, we spotted Ginger. We were so excited to see him again! We called out to him, "Ginger, Ginger, vieni qua!" ("Come here!") To our surprise and delight, he came! Immediately, he ran to me and pushed his head back and forth against my hand and started sucking my finger. By now his teeth were really growing and they pricked me. I didn't mind, though, because I was just so happy that he remembered his "Momma"!

We looked and looked for Bo, but couldn't find him anywhere. When we asked about him, the shepherd told us some very sad news: Bo didn't make it. He was too sick and weak and eventually died. Our hearts were so broken. Dear little Bo—the crybaby—gone.

Ginger, on the other hand, was doing well. The first few weeks we saw him, he just wanted to stay close to us. Oh, it was so cute, but we quickly realized that he needed to be with the rest of the flock more than he needed to be with us. It was so hard convincing him to stop sucking our finger but to instead go and eat real food with the rest of the flock.

Over the last few evenings, however, something has been changing. He comes to me, sucks briefly on my finger with his prickly little teeth, and then quickly runs back to eat the grass with the rest of the flock. In some ways this saddens me, but I know that it is the best thing for him. He is now truly a part of the flock and is closely following the shepherd. I can see that Ginger is eventually going to grow into an adult and one day have babies of his own.

What a moving illustration this is of spiritual birth and maturity! It is always so exciting when someone decides to follow Jesus, our Good Shepherd. It is very similar to a new little lamb that is born into a flock. Just as my girls and I did with Ginger and Bo, we Christians need to feed these "infants in Christ" the pure spiritual milk of the Word, that they may grow up in their salvation. While we may need to help clean away some of the filth of the world that is still clinging to them, it is also important that we encourage them and show them Christian love. Moreover, there will be moments of distraction and confusion as they are learning to follow the Good Shepherd on their own. Therefore, it is vital that we teach them to follow Him closely.

At first, they may depend on us a lot in order to survive spiritually, but after we have done our part, we need to let them go. We need to surrender them to our Good Shepherd and trust that they will learn to follow Him on their own. Of course, this doesn't mean that we abandon them, it just means they need to learn to mature and eat the solid food of the Word on their own instead of being fed milk in a bottle all their lives!

It is important to be aware, however, that not all of them will make it, even if we do everything right. When I think about Ginger and Bo, it reminds me of what Jesus said in the Parable of the Sower. Many who come to Christ receive the Word with joy, but not all will come to the point of Christian maturity where they will bear spiritual fruit. Both Ginger and Bo wagged their tails with joy as they guzzled down that warm milk. We nurtured both of them equally and still, one made it and the other didn't.

Even though it's hard to think about having lost Bo, we find great joy in knowing that Ginger is getting bigger, stronger, and healthier by the day. He, like the other adult sheep, dedicates his time to constantly eating solid food and following the shepherd closely. I have no doubt that he will one day bring new life into the flock. How wonderful it is knowing that we had a part in bringing him to that place!

May each one of us, in turn, bring new life into *God's* flock. As we help people come to a decision to follow Christ, may we nurture them, love them, and teach them. Then, when it is time to let go, may we release them into the care of our Good Shepherd. In the end, we will rejoice in those who make it to full spiritual maturity. What satisfaction it will be for us, knowing that they will remember us as their spiritual parents! Furthermore, as we see them follow our Good Shepherd and bring new life to His flock, this will be our great reward!

"Do not be afraid, little flock, for your Father has been pleased to give you the kingdom." —Luke 12:32

CHAPTER 14

BEHOLD! THE LAMB OF GOD!

Remember those twin preemie lambs we had at our home for a couple of days? They were so adorable! My girls and I were looking forward to lots of cuddles with them. . . . *but*, there was a bit of a problem! It seems they had some diarrhea trouble which caused their back ends to be crusted with filth. (Not exactly the perfect conditions for cuddling!)

Bo was a little white lamb—and also a terrible crybaby! If he was hungry, he'd cry. If he saw us go inside, he'd cry. If he simply wanted to be near us, he'd cry. It seemed like all that little guy ever did was cry!

And then it came time to give Bo his bath. He had never had one before, so I could only imagine how much he was going to cry. I also figured he would put up quite a fight. I put him into the small basin filled with warm sudsy water. The poor little fellah had no idea what was happening to him! I could feel his heart beating wildly as I pressed his little body into the water until his entire body was submerged. The surprising thing, though, was that he never let out one cry! He never kicked one hoof. He never even struggled to get free. He just lay there silently—in total surrender—even though he was so afraid!

It was at that very moment that I understood what the Bible said about Jesus when He died on the cross for our sins. He could have struggled. He could have cried out. He could have called on thousands of angels to save Him from that horrid death on the cross. But the Bible says, "He was led like a lamb to the slaughter, and as a sheep before its shearers is silent, so he did not open his mouth" (Isaiah 53:7).

As I looked at Bo—that perfect little white lamb—lying there in complete surrender, I finally understood why John the Baptist cried out, "Behold, the Lamb of God, who takes away the sin of the world!" (John 1:29, ESV)

Jesus—although He was without sin—laid down His life as a sacrifice to pay the price for our sins, once and for all. He willingly did this because of His great love for you and for me! Watching that little lamb that day, I came to appreciate in an even greater way the tremendous love of Jesus—the *perfect* Lamb of God.

We all, like sheep, have gone astray, each of us has turned to our own way; and the LORD has laid on him the iniquity of us all. —Isaiah 53:6

CHAPTER 15

I JUST WANT TO BE A SHEEP

When I first met the shepherd, I asked him about the verses in the Bible that talk about how Jesus will one day separate the sheep from the goats. I had seen him do the same thing. I asked him why.

I will never forget his answer: "Goats are so much harder to take care of. They don't listen to my voice. They do what they want. They are always in trouble. Look at the sheep. They keep their heads to the ground, contentedly eating the grass I have led them to. The goats always have their heads up. They are looking around, always wanting something different to eat; always going astray."

I have watched them! The goats are always wandering off! Always in search of what they are not supposed to have . . . and never satisfied. At times, the goats even lead the sheep astray!

I would like to share this dramatic account of the goats' disobedience to illustrate this point:

The shepherd called out to the flock. He was directing them to follow him into the next field. The sheep were right behind him. The goats had another idea, however. Instead of listening to the shepherd, they ran into the street. The shepherd called out to them, but they wouldn't listen. They spitefully ran away from him. We had to walk quickly—well, as quickly as an eighty-eight-year-old shepherd can walk! When we reached them, they came back to the edge of the field, only to start running again.

The shepherd turned to me and said, "Look at them! They're going to go all the way back there where the people throw out their food." Sure enough, they stopped where he said they would. We finally reached them another time. Just as soon as we did, they ran off once again! "I capri sono briganti!!!" ("The goats are troublemakers!"), he exclaimed.

"They're going to go to the apple tree," he explained, "right down there before the road." Just then they stopped in the field. "Oh yes," he said, "there is another pile over there where the people throw out their rotten fruits and vegetables." We continued chasing the goats as the shepherd called out to them to stop. I couldn't believe my eyes as they looked back at the shepherd and defiantly made their way back into the street only a couple minutes after he had stopped them! A car came and had to wait a few seconds until they passed by. At this, the shepherd was furious! He threw his staff at them and they ran back into the field.

By now I was feeling pretty bad for the shepherd. Those goats just kept running away from him! I had been spending a lot of time with him and had seen the bad behavior of the goats on many other occasions, but never had I seen the goats disobey him this badly!

"*Now* they're headed to that apple tree," the shepherd said. No matter what the shepherd did, those goats were determined to go where they wanted to go and to do what they wanted to do! This time the shepherd had a plan. He and I made it to the apple tree before the goats did, which prevented them from going any farther. Finally, the poor shepherd could get some rest!

The shepherd and I sat on the edge of the little canal like we so often do, talking about the sheep, talking about life. I thanked him for coming over for lunch that day. He told me he really enjoyed the cheesecake.

Just then, we looked out at the flock. At that moment I made a great observation: "This whole time, the goats have been running away from you, but the sheep have been quietly following you." We both looked out to see that the sheep had quietly followed him the whole way and were contentedly eating in the field, just like he had said to me many years earlier. The goats, on the other hand, had already left the apple tree and were already headed back in the same direction from which they had come. They crossed the street and ate some people's bushes. The shepherd had to make his grunts to make them stop. After a while, they finally listened to him. Then they jumped into the street just as a car came by. I had to laugh at those naughty goats!

Well, it was getting late, so I said goodbye to the shepherd. He thanked me for coming out to be with him. As I walked back home, I found some of those goats in our yard eating our bushes! I gently smacked their behinds and told them to go back to the shepherd. Just then, an onlooker said, "It's just like the saying: 'As wayward as a goat!'"

After seeing all the drama that evening, I couldn't agree more with that saying!

Some great observations I have made: The goats are always running away from the shepherd, while the sheep quietly follow him. Likewise, the goats even lead their children astray, but the sheep keep their children close to the shepherd.

I want to be like a sheep. To be happy in Jesus—and close to my Good Shepherd. Content to feed in the green pastures He has led me to. I want to know His voice. To listen to Him ... and to obey.

"... his sheep follow him because they know his voice." —John 10:4

CHAPTER 16

THE SHEPHERDESS

had an exciting new experience today! It was just me and the whole flock of 150 sheep and goats. I was a shepherdess!

Over the past five years, I had been spending lots of time with my elderly shepherd friend. I had been given many fantastic opportunities to observe him and help him with his flock. I figured I had learned all there was to know about leading a flock and I was feeling pretty confident. So much so that I had a little secret desire: to be alone with the flock so I could see what it was like to be a shepherdess!

Today I got my wish. As I was out in the field taking pictures of the sheep, the shepherd came up to me and told me he had to go away for an hour. He asked me if I would look after the sheep. At that moment they were resting in a patch of woods between two fields. He told me that he would take them into the next field when he came back. Until then, he thought they should stay put in the shade of the woods. He instructed me to call him if the flock started moving and he would come back right away.

At last, I was going to be able to prove that *I* could take care of the sheep—without the shepherd's help! It seemed easy enough. I wanted to tell him, "I've been watching you and helping you all these years and now I know all there is to know. I can do it myself!" Instead, I just answered with an eager, "Yes!" and then he went away.

At first, the animals were just resting, so I continued taking pictures. I loved how I was able to be so close to the sheep while I was taking their pictures! I used to just frighten them away if I got too close to them. Now, after several years, I had finally won their trust. I continued to click away.

Just then, I saw some movement and realized that a few of the goats had stood up—and then started wandering off! I went to call the shepherd only to learn that I had forgotten my cell phone. *Oh no! What do I do now?* There was nothing left to do but run and try to cut them off before they got into the road. I went quickly, but one darted ahead of me. I tried making the shepherd's guttural noise, "Geh!" The flock knows me by now, but they also know that I am *not* the shepherd! My "geh" noise isn't quite as effective as it is when the shepherd does it. I jumped up the little hill and chased that goat down right before he got into the street. I also shooed the rest of the goats back to the flock. I did it! All of the flock was back together.

After that little incident, I went to see Ginger, a little lamb that we had helped the shepherd bottle-feed. He came to cuddle with me. While I was petting him, I noticed that—*oh no!*—the goats were *all* running out of the field! This time they were going the other way and were already next to the street. Once again, I made the shepherd's deep "geh" noise. Some pulled back, but others kept going into the street. I thought, "What would the shepherd do?" I remembered that when he couldn't get to the goats or sheep in time, he often threw his staff or a stick out by them to show them he meant business. Somehow, between my guttural noise and the tossed stick, those goats actually got the message. They turned around and headed back to the rest of the flock! I was so proud of myself!

I strutted back to the wooded area and found little Ginger. I called him back to me and he came scurrying. "Did you see me, Ginger?" I exclaimed, "*I* am a *shepherdess*! I got all of those goats to come back . . . *all by myself!*" And just while I was in the middle of boasting, I saw that the goats were beginning to stray again—and this time they were even taking some of the sheep with them! Worse yet, they were all headed *in the wrong direction*!

I ran to try to stop them from going any farther. I managed to stop them, but when I looked back, I saw that some others were getting ready to dash into the street! Once again, I went running. I cut them off before they got into the street, but then noticed that others were now headed in *another* direction! I ran and shouted, "Geh!" until the goats were all back with the rest of the sheep.

By now, the entire flock was through resting. They were all standing and ready to go into the next field. The shepherd still had not returned. I knew he had said that he was going to take them to the next field when he got back, so I ran behind them to try to get them to head in the right direction—and to block them from going the opposite way. Then I had to run to the left of the flock to keep them from going out into the road. It was quite a challenge! I had to be very careful with my movements so I wouldn't divide the flock. I was pretty much running circles around them. (No, I had never seen the shepherd do that before, but I was getting kind of desperate!) It was the only thing I could do to keep them all from scattering! For the next fifteen-or-so minutes, I was running this way and that, trying to keep the 150-member flock together.

I really hated to admit it, but at that moment I realized that when I walked with the shepherd close by my side, we *led* the flock! Without him I was using all of my time and strength just trying to keep the flock together and out of trouble!

After some time, I had managed to get the entire flock in the same field. And then—*finally*—the shepherd came back! When he did, he found his flock rather spread out all over the field—but at least they were out of the street and all in the correct field! He also found a *very* exhausted shepherdess!

I discovered something that day: I *need* the shepherd's help. I can't do it alone. And that's exactly how it is in life. I can't do it alone. I need the help of Jesus, my Good Shepherd.

How many of us have wanted to try to do things on our own at one time or another? Though we may not voice it, we pull away from God, and our actions declare to Him, "I don't need you in my life. I can do this myself!" We think we know all there is to know about life. I realize that occasionally we may actually do an okay job without Him. And when that happens, we become proud. Sooner or later, though, we find ourselves running in circles. Exhausted. And only doing a second-rate job. That's because when I choose to be in charge of my life, I do everything in my own strength. I yield mediocre results and quickly grow weary. If, however, I choose to walk with the Shepherd at my side in all I do, *He* does what I cannot do. The job is much easier. I am rested. With His help and guidance, I can do an excellent job. You see, He never meant for us to do it alone. Walking with the Good Shepherd makes *all* the difference in life!

So now I understand that maybe being a shepherdess *isn't* really all that important. Maybe I *don't* want to do it on my own. Maybe I'd rather just continue walking *with* the shepherd.

"Come to me, all you who are weary and burdened, and I will give you rest. Take my yoke upon you and learn from me, for I am gentle and humble in heart, and you will find rest for your souls. For my yoke is easy and my burden is light." —Matthew 11:28-30

CHAPTER 17
WHERE IS HE?

"I'm going to bring two ice pops tonight," I told my husband. "That way I can show the shepherd how to eat an ice pop while he is eating his." It was the middle of August and we were in the middle of two weeks of upper 90s and 100 degrees. I couldn't even imagine how a shepherd who was eighty-eight years old could even bear being in that heat. I decided to bring him some cold water each evening. After about a week, I had the brilliant idea of bringing him an ice pop! Just the night before I brought him our last one. He had never even seen one before and had no idea how to eat it! I chuckled to myself as he folded down the plastic as if it were a banana peel. I determined that we would buy more right away and that the next evening I would eat one with him!

Equipped with a bottle of ice water and two ice pops, I left the house. The sheep were directly in front of our house so I figured he must be pretty close by. I looked in the field where the sheep were coming from, but he wasn't there. My husband told me there were some sheep in the other field, so we went out there. I know all the shady spots where he sits, so I went to each one, but he wasn't in any of those places. At that moment, as I was standing still, I heard a distant call. "I think I heard him," I said to my husband. We looked around everywhere, but he was simply nowhere to be found.

I realized that I was going to have to cross both of the fields and go over to the wooded area where he often watches over the sheep. It was strange, though, because he didn't usually stay there when the sheep came all the way into this field. It was going to take a lot longer to get to him than I had thought. By now, the ice pops were melting. Losing hope of reaching him in time to eat them with him, I ended up eating them both.

Following the road, I scanned all the nearby fields. I knew he had to be somewhere nearby, but I didn't see him. Just then I was hit with an awful thought, *what if something had happened to him?* He is, after all, an elderly man, and this heat wave has been draining him of his strength. I turned into the wooded area and walked faster and faster trying to get to the end where he often sits. I called out to him, but there was no response.

A sheep with her little lambs came running out and joined the half of the flock that was in the nearby field. *What would happen to the flock if something happened to him,* I wondered . . . *what would happen . . . to me?* Not only has he come to enjoy my visits, my help, and my refreshments, but I have come to enjoy these special moments with my shepherd friend. It was a lonely feeling thinking of not having him there. I quickly dismissed those sad thoughts and continued to search for him. No matter how much I searched, he simply wasn't there. He wasn't anywhere. But how was that possible? He *had* to be there! His sheep needed him!

Sweat dripped from my brow as I scanned the next field. The grass and the ground were extremely dry from this hot spell. Trying to imagine where he might be, I realized something. The goats were missing, too! Now I understood everything. The goats must have gone astray and the shepherd had to go after them. The goats have certain areas where they wander to. I walked down the street where they often go, but the shepherd and the goats were nowhere to be found. After walking all the way back, I thought about something the shepherd had said just the other day. He said that the goats had wandered all the way down another field that was hardly visible. I made my way down there. My husband joined me as we walked.

"Look, I see the goats!" I said to him.

Right behind the goats, under a shady tree, was a beautiful sight. The shepherd, with his white hair and staff in hand, stood to greet us. He waved at us and smiled. I had never been so happy to see him!

When we finally reached him, he explained, "The goats came all the way here so I had to come and be with them."

"I'm sorry it's not very cold anymore," I said to him as I gave him the water. "We've been looking everywhere for you, but we couldn't find you."

After he had finished guzzling down some water, he answered, "I know. I saw you in that field. I even called out to you. Then I saw you go to the trees and then I saw you coming over here."

We walked back to the rest of the flock with the goats. As we passed by my house, I told him, "Oh, wait here, I need to get something!" Running into the house, I got two more ice pops. I quickly ran back outside. We sat in the shade and I showed him how to squeeze the ice up and suck the juice out. He pushed his up and it almost popped out. We both laughed together.

I touched his hand and said, "You really had me scared today. I'm so glad you're okay." He smiled at me.

Just then, I realized that while I was so worried and looking for him, he was there the whole time, watching over the flock . . . even watching me!

God showed me something that day. We have all gone through—or will go through—dry spells. There may be days—even seasons—when God, our Good Shepherd, seems so far away. When we search and search for Him, but simply can't see Him. We may wonder why He is no longer right beside us and we may be filled with loneliness. When we call out to Him, we may not hear Him. But if we are still— if we stop and listen carefully—we just might hear that still, small voice reassuring us that He *is* there. You see, just like my shepherd friend, God is far enough away not to be seen, yet close enough to see everything. He is our Good Shepherd, always watching over us; ever ready to come to our aid. If we continue to seek Him, we will surely find Him! And then, when we are finally sitting in His presence once again, we will laugh together with joy!

You, God, are my God, earnestly I seek you; I thirst for you, my whole being longs for you, in a dry and parched land where there is no water. —Psalm 63:1

CHAPTER 18

MERCY MIXED WITH FEAR

By now, the bleating of sheep has become a familiar sound to our ears. The shepherd comes by our home with his flock of sheep, leading them from one pasture to another. One morning my husband was outside and called out to me saying, "There's a sheep with her lamb out in the field, but I can't see the shepherd anywhere. They're wandering from field to field and don't know how to get back to the shepherd."

I can't tell you how much I love to go and rescue little lambs! The ultimate experience is when I get to hold one in my arms, but it's really hard to catch them, so that doesn't happen very often.

I promptly left the house and headed into the field, thinking of my strategy to return the lost sheep and her lamb to the shepherd. I would try to scoop up the lamb and carry it ahead of the sheep, hopefully persuading it to follow us to the shepherd. I walked out to the middle of the field. Just as my husband had said, there was the sheep with her little two-day-old lamb—I mean—lambs. Oh, I hadn't counted on twins. This was going to be a lot harder than I had anticipated! I approached the ewe cautiously, knowing that sheep are usually quite afraid of anyone except the shepherd. I talked to her in soothing Italian words. Somehow, she actually allowed me to get near her babies. I was surprised at how easily I was able to get a hold of the first lamb, but trying to catch the other with one already in my hands was a lot more difficult! I started thinking that maybe I had gotten in over my head. As I went to grab the second lamb, I noticed that it was much skinnier than the other. Actually, I've never seen such a scrawny lamb before. I seized it and managed to get it into my other arm, holding both of the lambs with their heads facing forward.

I started walking in the shepherd's direction very slowly, hoping that the mother would follow us. . . . and after one of her babies let out a little cry, she did! Normally, the sheep run away from us, but this one was actually following me! My plan had worked! By then, I was feeling just a *little* bit proud. *I* did it! *I* captured both of those little lambs all by myself and I was going to bring them back to the shepherd with their mamma following behind! Just then, I stepped into a hole, and down I tumbled, lambs and all. I found myself fallen, on my back, feet up, still holding the lambs in my arms! At first, I couldn't even figure out how to get back up. I'm sure that ewe was saying, "And *you* are supposed to be saving *us*?"

I propped myself up with my elbows and eventually got myself back on my feet. I looked around to see if anyone had witnessed that beautiful show and yes—of course—there was a witness. *Wonderful*. Oh well.

Off we continued on our journey back to the shepherd. The mother followed us for a while, but then something spooked her and off she went, running—as fast as she could—in the opposite direction! Mamma mia, what was I going to do now? Just then, I noticed that my husband was nearby walking the dog. I asked him to block the sheep. That in and of itself was another interesting little show. He jumped this way and that and finally got her to go in the right direction. Once again, we were all back together. The little lambs were in my arms, their *baaing* was encouraging the mother sheep to follow us back to the shepherd and I was having thoughts of household salvation: bringing the entire family to the Good Shepherd. How moving!

Well, that lasted for about two minutes. For the next fifteen minutes, the mother sheep would run off in another direction, then one of the lambs would call out, and the mother would come back. Just when I thought we were going to get her to return to the shepherd with us, she would turn away again. This happened over and over again!

At one point, I myself was a little confused about the shepherd's location. If I didn't know where he was, how was I going to bring these little lambs back to him? My husband called out to me, "I saw him. He's over there in that other field." Okay, at least we were going in the right direction now.

By then, I was getting pretty tired. I made a *baaing* noise myself, which roused one of the little lambs to *baa*. This, in turn, caused the mother to come back. We were getting closer to the shepherd and I thought we just might make it when the mother took off in a panic. She went running this way and that. She went behind someone's house and took off in another direction. We were so sad, but we had done all we could do. It seemed there was no hope of us leading her to the shepherd now. We had no other choice but to bring the lambs back without their mother.

Meanwhile, the twins were cuddling in my arms, one with its head on top of the other. Every once in a while, one would suckle my finger. As I continued walking to the shepherd the little lambs got so heavy that I had to reposition them, placing one with its head up over my shoulder. I noticed that the one looked so weak. His brother held his head straight up, while he laid with his head hanging over my arms. I was pretty worried about him.

I crossed the large field that would eventually lead us back to the shepherd. My husband had the dog so he couldn't help me with the lambs. I asked him to try to get my hair out of my face. I was sweaty and dirty and the lambs' hooves had scratched my arms and my neck. The worst thing, though, was that I had the filth of the lambs all over my arms and my chest and I stunk! My arms were getting so weak. I wasn't sure I'd make it all the way back to the shepherd, but I knew that if I put the lambs down now, they'd just go running in any direction. I *had* to keep going. I *had* to get them back to the shepherd! Just then, I saw the rest of the flock. When I saw the shepherd, I was given renewed strength. I kept my eyes on him. I was going to get back to him no matter what it took!

Within minutes, we were finally back with the shepherd. Can you imagine our surprise when we returned to see that the mother sheep had already returned to him? Apparently, she had seen her need for him and somehow found her way back on her own! It was a happy reunion for all.

I wondered, though . . . how could a mother and her lambs end up so far away from the rest of the flock? The shepherd told me that when they had left the pen early that morning, the mother had only one of her twins with her since the other one was so weak. She didn't want it to die, so she decided to leave the shepherd and return to the pen to get her other baby. In doing so, she and the stronger lamb ended up getting separated from the shepherd and the rest of the flock.

I wasn't going to write a story about this incident. However, while I was praying and reading my Bible that day, God showed me that there was something very important to learn from this story.

That mother sheep and I are like Christians with unbelieving friends whom they hope to lead to—or bring back to—the Good Shepherd. This can be a wonderful thing. However, it can be dangerous if you go too far into the world and allow these relationships to pull you away from your Good Shepherd. You may find yourself like that well-intentioned mother. She thought it was the best thing to leave the shepherd so she could save her baby. In doing so, however, not only did she find herself lost, but she inevitably led her other baby away from the shepherd as well. You may also find yourself in way over your head like me with those little twin lambs and their mother. But then, things may really start to work out and you might start feeling proud of the work you are doing for the Good Shepherd. If you're not careful, though, you may begin to think that you are standing firm and that *nothing* could make you fall into sin. And then, never seeing it coming, you may find yourself fallen—flat on your back—wondering how you are ever going to get back up.

So, does this mean that we should not spend any time with people who are not Christians? Of course not. We are called to go out and seek and save the lost sheep. However, we *do* need to be on guard! As it says in the book of Jude, we need to "show mercy, mixed with fear." In reaching out to them, we need to keep a safe distance from their sin so that we will not be "stained" by it. We also need to remember to stay close to our Good Shepherd. Otherwise, we may not only find ourselves separated from Him, but we may also lead *others* astray. Most of all, we need to remember to keep our eyes on Him. If we do, He will show us the way. He will give us the strength to stand firm and not fall as we gather the lambs in our arms. Not only will we enjoy His good pasture, but we will be able to carry many others to the Shepherd and Overseer of our souls.

And have mercy on some, who are doubting; save others, snatching them out of the fire; and on some have mercy with fear, hating even the garment polluted by the flesh. Now to Him who is able to protect you from stumbling, and to make you stand in the presence of His glory blameless with great joy, to the only God our Savior, through Jesus Christ our Lord, be glory, majesty, dominion and authority, before all time and now and forever. Amen. —Jude 1:22-25

CHAPTER 19

THE SHEPHERD'S TOUCH

t was a cold winter evening. When I went out to walk the dog, I saw that my shepherd friend was nearby. Instead of taking the dog down the road, I decided to take her down the path that led to the shepherd and his sheep so I could wish him a happy New Year.

As I walked down the path, I saw a mother sheep with her two newborn lambs. One lamb was standing and nursing while the other was just lying on the ground with his neck sort of twisted. I wondered if he was dead. I looked a little longer and saw him move, so I continued down the path to the shepherd. We wished each other a happy New Year, greeting each other with the traditional kiss on each cheek.

We talked for some time and then I asked him about the twin lambs I had seen. He said they had been born just a couple of hours earlier. I asked if something was wrong with the one with the twisted neck, but he said it would be fine. After we had talked a little longer, I started to make my way back down the path.

While I did, I decided to look in on the little lamb. He was still lying there with his neck twisted. I crossed over the canal to get a better look. I went over to him and touched him. He was barely breathing and looked lifeless. I could see that, although his sister was all cleaned up by her mother, he hadn't even been cleaned yet. He lay there shivering, wet and cold. I remembered that the shepherd had once told me that it was very important for mothers to clean their lambs right away in the wintertime. Otherwise, they might die.

"He looks so weak," I called out to the shepherd.

He seemed not to hear . . . or not to care. "Are you sure he's okay?" I asked.

He still didn't say anything. I was sure I must be getting on his nerves going on about this little lamb, but I was genuinely concerned. Without his intervention, I was sure that this sweet little lamb was going to die ... and soon! So I persisted, "His mother hasn't cleaned him up yet ... and he's trembling."

I'm not sure if it was because I wouldn't give up or if it was the pleading look in my eyes, but at that moment the shepherd began to move toward me and the little lamb. He shook him and then he picked him up and carried him over the canal into the next field. His mother and sister followed. The shepherd rubbed the little lamb. He lifted him to his feet and he stood for the first time. All of a sudden, the little lamb was filled with life! His mother started cleaning him and then the little lamb walked over to her and began nursing for the first time.

I was so happy I didn't give up! Now I could go back home in peace. As I walked, I thought about how the shepherd's touch had made all the difference—it brought life!

Are you at that place where you know that without the touch of Jesus, our Good Shepherd, there is no hope? Do you find yourself pleading with Him and wondering if He hears you? Jesus said that if we ask, it *will* be given to us. But what if it seems like He doesn't even care? He says that if we seek, we *will* find. And when He is silent? Sure, we may think we are bothering Him as we continue to implore Him with our prayers, but He, Himself, told us to knock—to *keep* knocking—and the door *will* be opened! When He sees our persistence, His heart will be touched. It is then that He will move toward us. He will lift us to our feet and work like only He can do! So don't stop praying! Keep asking! Keep seeking! Keep knocking! In the end, we will see that He *does* hear and that He *does* care! But most of

all, we will see that the Shepherd's touch makes *all* the difference...
it brings *life* to a hopeless situation!

---

*"Ask and it will be given to you; seek and you
will find; knock and the door will be opened to
you. For everyone who asks receives; the one
who seeks finds; and to the one who knocks,
the door will be opened."* —Matthew 7:7-8

CHAPTER 20

HE'S NEVER COMING BACK!

Driving back home onto our dead-end road one day, my husband and I found the flock of sheep scattered all over two fields. I looked for the shepherd but he was gone. He had apparently left them alone for some time in one of the fields. He very rarely does this, but if he does, he has certain expectations, the greatest being, "Don't go astray!" I'm sure those sheep stayed where he left them for some time but started thinking after a while, *He's never coming back!* By the time we got to them, there were only a few sheep left where the shepherd had left them. The rest were running around in another field, carefree and in total disobedience! The shepherd was nowhere in sight and they were living their lives however they pleased.

Of course, they weren't considering the fact that they depend on the shepherd for *everything*! He is their provider, their leader, their protector, their rescuer, their helper—and not to mention—the one who keeps them out of trouble!

We stopped the car by some of the sheep that had gone into the road. I looked at them as if to say, "Go back! The shepherd will be returning soon!" Some of the sheep went back into the field, but others (especially the goats) defiantly remained in the middle of the road.

Just then, the unexpected happened: that ninety-year-old shepherd, with his beautiful white hair, came back suddenly, riding on a white—*bicycle*!!! (True story.)

I really wish you could have seen the sheep who had gone astray. As *one*, they went running violently! They knew they would be in trouble if they were caught, but they thought they might be able to beat him back to the other field! Try as they might, however, they were not fast enough. The shepherd returned to find that only a few had remained obedient. He was angry with the rest of the sheep and he gave them a harsh rebuke!

I had to laugh at those foolish sheep, running as fast as they could, thinking they could outsmart the shepherd. I laughed, but then I became very sober as I thought about us as sheep. Aren't we kind of the same way? Sometimes we think that Jesus, our Good Shepherd, is never coming back! But He has promised that He *will* come back one day! Now, He may not come back riding a white bicycle, but someday He *will* come back riding a white horse! No one knows the day or the hour.

All I can say is, whether I meet Him when He comes back in the clouds, on a white horse, or if I meet Him through death, I just want to be ready! I don't want to be like those sheep saying, "He's never coming back!" and then live whatever kind of life I want to live. In doing so, I would be forgetting how much I need Him and that, even if I can't see Him, He is watching over me. He sees what I am doing—even when no one else is around. I need to always remember that today is the day I could meet Him. I want to be ready for that day ... how about you?

---

*"Therefore keep watch, because you
do not know on what day your Lord
will come."*—Matthew 24:42

CHAPTER 21

UP AGAINST A WALL

Autumn had come to Italy. On this one beautiful evening, I was enjoying spending some time with my shepherd friend. We were talking in the middle of a field, surrounded by the flock of sheep. Just then, the shepherd got up abruptly and said it was time to lead the sheep into another field. They had been in that field for some time now, so it was time to move on to a field with fresher grass.

Normally the sheep would be quick to follow the shepherd, but at that moment something odd happened. There was a concrete wall at the end of the field. Instead of turning right to follow the shepherd, the sheep just kept advancing toward the wall. It wasn't out of disobedience; they simply thought that they should continue going in that direction, despite the shepherd's voice beckoning them to change their course and come into a new field!

I'm not sure how to describe that scene, but as one, the flock of over a hundred sheep kept thrusting themselves into the wall. As the sheep in the back got closer to the wall the flock looked as though it was shrinking. They continued to press closer and closer, almost climbing on each other's backs trying to go forward! The shepherd attempted to get their attention by making some noises, but they didn't hear him. Apparently, they were too busy trying to push down that wall!

At one point they were so compressed that they were no longer able to move. Now you'd think at least some of them might have gotten a clue that something was wrong by now! Maybe someone would have said, "Hey guys, this isn't working very well. I think we need to reconsider our plan. By the way . . . does anyone hear what the shepherd is trying to tell us?" But remember, sheep are dumb. They simply kept trying to press forward. I stood there watching this incredible sight, wondering if some of them might get trampled.

At last, some of the sheep started paying attention to the shepherd's voice. When they finally figured it out, they saw that the shepherd had *another* plan that did not involve them being crushed! His plan was to lead them to a fresh, green field!

He had been there all along, calling out to them, but it was only when they stopped and listened for his voice that they could hear him clearly and know which direction to go in.

There are times in our lives when we think we are supposed to go in one direction, but God, our Good Shepherd, is calling us to go in another. Sometimes He closes a door or even puts up a wall along our path. That's because He has another plan—a *better* plan! Meanwhile, He beckons us to come and follow Him, but we may be so busy that we can't hear His voice. We may also think *our* way is better. We may push forward and wonder why we are getting nowhere. We may feel like we are being crushed, or like we are up against a wall. (Do we really think we can make that wall move?) In the process, we may be hurting ourselves—and others!

If we would just stop and listen to His still, small voice, we would hear Him saying, "Come . . . *this* way . . . follow me." If we'd listen even further, we'd hear that voice saying, "I have great plans for your life—plans to bless you and not to harm you. I want to give you hope and a future."

It is so important that we remember that His ways are high above our ways. We need to follow Him even when it doesn't make sense. If we will surrender to *His* plan for our lives and *trust* Him, we will see that He is leading us into fresher, greener pastures. When we look back one day, we will realize that He knew what was best for us all along!

It's all about trusting Him, listening to His voice, letting go of our own plans . . . and saying yes to His!

"For I know the plans I have for you," declares the Lord, *"plans to prosper you and not to harm you, plans to give you hope and a future. Then you will call on me and come and pray to me, and I will listen to you. You will seek me and find me when you seek me with all your heart."*—Jeremiah 29:11-13

CHAPTER 22
THE ADOPTION

My shepherd friend and I were sitting on the edge of a small canal that divides two fields. He often sits on these canals or on a tree stump. After all, where else do you sit while you are out in the fields all day with the sheep? While we were sitting there quietly, I looked out at the flock. Most of them were grazing, but a few lambs were running and playing in the distance.

As I studied the flock further, I noticed that one of the sheep looked significantly different than the rest. Her ears were floppier and pinker than the others. Her wool was fluffier and silkier, too. I asked the shepherd about her.

The shepherd told me her story....

Somewhere in the mountains was another shepherd with another flock of sheep. His sheep were of a different breed. They didn't look like his. Besides that, they grazed up in the mountains, rather than in the outskirts of the city. The mountain shepherd had brought his sheep down into the valley to graze. During that time, a sheep strayed from his flock. When the shepherd gathered his flock to bring them back up the mountain, the stray sheep was nowhere to be found. As a result, she got left behind. By the time someone found her, she was filthy. She was alone. She was desperately lost and without her shepherd. Her rescuers searched and searched for her shepherd, but he had returned with his flock up into the mountains and they had no way of finding him.

Someone told them about my shepherd friend. They decided to bring the sheep to him. I can't imagine how difficult it must have been for them to get this big sheep to the shepherd! Most people do not have trucks in Italy, so it is very possible they stuffed her in their car! The thought of it makes me laugh. Oh, what a terrific odor that must have remained in their vehicle!

When the shepherd got her, he cleaned her up and helped her feel better. He lovingly took her and adopted her into his own flock, treating her like one of his very own sheep. Moreover, the entire flock welcomed her as one of them. She has learned to follow the shepherd just as they do. She has even borne sheep into the shepherd's flock! To this very day, she is a part of the shepherd's family of sheep!

You know, I, too, was like that lost sheep! My heart was filthy with sin. I felt alone and so desperately lost. And then someone brought me to Jesus, my Good Shepherd!

How wonderful it is that He accepts each and every one of us into His flock! It doesn't matter where we come from or what we look like. Our Good Shepherd shows no partiality! He loves us all the same! He graciously takes us into His arms and cleans us up. He heals our wounds and teaches us to follow Him.

We are lovingly adopted into the family of God!

He predestined us to adoption as sons through Jesus Christ to Himself, according to the kind intention of His will, to the praise of the glory of His grace, which He freely bestowed on us in the Beloved. —Ephesians 1:5-6, NASB

CHAPTER 23

WALKING UPRIGHTLY

There are few things more enjoyable than going for a walk in the Italian countryside. One evening I was out for a walk and as I passed by the sheep pen, I saw the shepherd doing something to one of his sheep.

"Buona sera!" ("Good evening!") I cried out. He answered but continued his work.

Curious, I walked down the narrow path that leads to the sheep pen so I could get a closer look at what he was doing. I asked him if I could come through the gate and he said yes. I carefully approached the shepherd so as not to disturb the sheep.

The shepherd was bent over his sheep, scraping away something from the sheep's hooves and then pouring something over them. Interestingly, the sheep completely surrendered to the shepherd and allowed him to do all that he needed to do.

I asked him what he was doing.

He said that he was scraping away the dirt, clipping the hooves, and pouring something on them to sanitize them. He explained that he needed to do this to his sheep because infection from their filth can come in through their feet. If left untreated, it could become an infection that would go all the way through their legs and affect the way they walk.

I didn't want to bother him too long, as it looked like he had a lot of work to do, but I thanked him for explaining it to me and wished him a good evening again.

As I made my way back onto the dirt road, I thought about what he was doing. It reminded me of the filth of this world that we walk through every day of our lives. If we don't allow our Good Shepherd to come and purify our hearts and our minds, those thoughts can turn into sin. If left untreated, it would be like an infection that grows in us, affecting the way we walk before the Lord.

Just as I witnessed that day, we need to allow our Good Shepherd to come and cleanse us and purge us of any filth that may have come into our lives. Like that sheep, if we will come to our Good Shepherd willingly, it won't hurt as much. But if we struggle, it might inflict more pain.

As we come to Him and allow Him to wash away our impurities, He makes us spiritually healthy and whole. As a result, we will then be able to walk before our Good Shepherd . . . with uprightness of heart.

Therefore, since we have these promises,
dear friends, let us purify ourselves
from everything that contaminates body
and spirit, perfecting holiness out of
reverence for God. —2 Corinthians 7:1

CHAPTER 24

YOU CAN MAKE IT!

Along the side of our home in Italy runs an old irrigation ditch that divides two fields. This canal often poses a challenge for the shepherd's flock as his sheep and goats have to jump over it to move from one field to the next. I must say, though, that it is a fascinating sight, watching 150 sheep and goats jumping over this obstacle until all have made it to the other side. It almost looks like a fluid movement as the flock crowds together and jumps over it!

Since I have mentioned how the sheep cross this canal in several of my shepherd stories, I decided that I should try to get some good pictures of this interesting event.

In order to do this, I looked out my window one afternoon, hoping to catch the shepherd as his sheep and goats leaped over the canal. They were still far off. I looked out a couple more times. One time when I looked out, I saw that the sheep had already begun crossing that ditch. The shepherd was standing beside them making sure they would make it over safely.

Camera in hand, I rushed out of the house and ran over to the field. After I had snapped a few shots of the leaping sheep, the shepherd went on ahead to the other side of the flock to keep the animals from going any farther.

While I was taking pictures of the sheep jumping over the canal two-by-two and four-by-four, a pair of twin lambs fell into the ditch. They looked toward the shepherd, crying out to him for help as they tried and tried to escape. After many futile attempts, they became exhausted. At that moment they stopped crying out; they stopped looking for the shepherd to come to their aid. Something notable is that once they took their eyes off the shepherd, their situation looked so hopeless to them. They felt like they couldn't get out on their own. Even though they knew they were supposed to follow the shepherd and the rest of the flock, they ended up simply giving up and lying down in the canal.

Just then, something very touching happened. All the sheep that were nearby—those who had just crossed the canal and those who were about to cross it—gathered around the lambs and surrounded them with a chorus of loud *baaing*. It was as though they were saying, "Hang in there! The shepherd will be coming to help you soon! Don't give up hope! You can make it!" They never left those little lambs. They kept on *baaing*, as if to cheer them on. To my surprise, their *baas* of encouragement made a huge difference! Those two discouraged lambs actually got back up on their feet! Once again, those little lambs started looking for the shepherd and calling out to him even louder with their high-pitched *baas*.

The shepherd heard the great commotion. He understood that the distressed *baaing* of those twin lambs was a cry for help. He swiftly made his way to them. Using his staff, he gently lifted them out of the canal. In an instant, everything was fine again! They were able to continue following the shepherd with the rest of the flock!

Have you ever been able to relate to those desperate little lambs that were stuck in the ditch? Maybe right now that's exactly how *you* feel! Everything seems so hopeless. You feel like you'll never make it and—just like those trapped lambs—you just want to lie down and never get back up. If that's you, I have a message for you: Don't be discouraged, help is on the way! If you will cry out to Jesus, our Good Shepherd, He will hear you. When your cry reaches His ears, He will come to your rescue! In an instant, your whole situation will turn around! Don't forget to keep your eyes on Jesus! When we take our eyes off our Good Shepherd, our circumstances always look more distressing. We end up seeing what *we* can do (not much), rather than what *Jesus* can do for us (a miracle)!

So don't give up! You can make it! A miracle is on the way!

Even if we can't relate to those little lambs right now, it is very likely that each one of us knows someone who is going through a hard time. Maybe someone has taken their eyes off the Good Shepherd. In doing so, they have become so overwhelmed by the obstacle in their way that everything looks hopeless to them. Their discouragement may even be so great that they are ready to let go of their faith. A great lesson to learn from this story is that our prayers and words of encouragement *do* have an effect! Not only did the *baaing* of the sheep encourage the lambs, but it also helped to get the shepherd's attention—just like our prayers! What a beautiful picture of the family of God!

It is our Good Shepherd's plan for us to be there for one another. Our prayers are so important. So are our words of encouragement! Even a simple sentence like, "You can make it!" or "I'm praying for you" can really help. Our uplifting words can restore hope. They can be the difference between somebody totally giving up or receiving new strength so that they can stand back up, fix their eyes on Jesus, and call out to Him once again until He comes and rescues them.

Is there someone around you who's going through a hard time? Let's ask God to show us how we can bring encouragement to them today!

Therefore encourage one another and build each other up, just as in fact you are doing. —1 Thessalonians 5:11

CHAPTER 25

WALKING WITH THE SHEPHERD AGAIN

Glancing out my window, I could see the sheep were following the shepherd. A few stray goats were in the road. One was even nibbling on our shrubs. This was a sight I had come to love over the last few years. Normally I would have run outside to greet the shepherd or even spent a little time with him and his sheep. But I was just so busy. Missions. The church. My family. Yes, they were all true needs, but still, I really did miss spending time with my shepherd friend.

I could tell that he, too, missed our time together. I would see him, whenever he passed by our home. He'd look over my way, waiting for me to run out of the house just as I had done so many times in the past years. Sometimes I'd peek out and wave at him, but it just wasn't the same.

One day I happened to be outside when he came by. I knew I had a lot to do, so I didn't talk to him long. I wanted to at least say hi, though. When I did, he said to me, "I saw you go away in your car yesterday."

Yes, I remembered. I saw him, too. I especially saw the way he looked at me, wishing I would just take a few minutes to come and talk to him . . . but I didn't come. He was watching. He was waiting. I was just. too. busy.

The months quickly passed and it was already winter. I realized I hadn't even seen the shepherd for a couple of weeks. How strange. I wondered if it was because this winter was especially cold in Italy. Maybe he had to keep the sheep in the pen and carry food to them or maybe he had them in the fenced-in field again, like he had during the heat of the summer.

Another week or two went by. By now I was really missing the shepherd. I missed hearing the bleating of sheep I had grown so accustomed to hearing.

It had now been several months since I had gone out to walk with the shepherd. At first my excuse for not going out to see him had been that I was too busy, then it was because it was too cold, and then because it snowed … and now … he just wasn't there anymore. Was it over? Was my friendship with him forever lost?

One day I was out walking the dog. I looked for the shepherd. I listened for the sheep. Oh, how I would have loved to see the shepherd that day! I missed my time with him. I missed our friendship.

As I walked by the fields, I remembered special moments we had shared together: silently walking together, laughing at the little lambs jumping in the fields, helping him rescue lost lambs. I remembered how he had picked me a pomegranate from a tree and how we would sit on the walls of the little canal and talk to each other. Other times we would just sit there together and enjoy each other's presence. When I walked with him daily, he had become like a father to me and even saw me as a daughter. Right now, it all seemed like a distant memory.

Every day I looked for the shepherd and listened for his sheep. I was determined that, even though I was still pretty busy, I was going to *make* the time to spend with him! That is, *if* he came back to the fields by our house. I looked for him; I listened and I waited. Another week went by. I knew that—no matter what I was doing—I would run out of the house if I so much as heard a little lamb's *baa*!

And then it happened. I was in the house and heard a soft jingle. Was I hearing things? There it was again! I remembered that the previous summer the shepherd had put a bell on one of the sheep. Was that the sheep's bell chiming? I threw on my coat and boots and dashed out of the house. I was thrilled to see the sheep entering the field in front of our home. (Many lambs had been born since I had last seen the flock!) The goats were sprawling all over our road (as usual) and the shepherd was right there beside them.

He smiled broadly at me. He walked as swiftly as a ninety-year-old man can walk and rushed out to meet me. He held out his arms and hugged me with a warm embrace. He was so happy! I was so happy! I was back with my shepherd friend and I knew that from here on out I would *find* time to be with him, no matter how busy life got!

This story is such a vivid picture of what can happen to us as Christians when we are walking with the Good Shepherd. Sometimes life gets busy. Our lives are full of commitments that can easily get in the way of our relationship with Jesus. However, if we're not careful, we may find ourselves making excuses as to why we can't meet with our Good Shepherd. We may miss our prayer time one day; we may not have time to read our Bible the next. Before we know it, maybe a week—or even more—has passed since we have had time with Him! We might pop in for prayer here and there with a little "Hello God!" but that just isn't the same. We must be very cautious, because this busyness can even affect our church attendance.

Yes, I know that most of us have very valid excuses. We're doing *good* things—very *important* things! But are they so important that they should replace our time with God?

In the end, we are left with an emptiness. We remember when we walked closely with our Good Shepherd, when we sat in His presence and listened to His voice, when we were filled with His love, joy, and peace. And now, He may seem so far away. We may even come to the realization that we are no longer walking with Him. We wonder how we ever got to where we are now . . . and how we can ever get back. We long to have that friendship with Him once again, but now, it only seems like a distant memory.

We are not the only ones who long to have that relationship restored. Our Good Shepherd yearns for the intimacy of our friendship. He is watching. He is waiting. Oh, how it must break His heart when He sees we are too busy for Him—that we have allowed all of these things to clutter our lives and get in the way of our walk with Him.

So how do we get back? We look for Him. We run to Him. We decide that no matter what comes in our lives, we *will* make that time for Him! The beautiful thing is, when we decide to turn back to Him, He will come running. Just like my shepherd friend, our Good Shepherd will hold us in His warm embrace with a smile on His face. His love for us is so great!

As I think about my life during that time, I can say that, yes, I *was* extremely busy. My needs *were* very real, but I also knew that once I started making excuses, it only became easier to make new ones. Looking back, I can see that if I had really wanted to, I could have found some time for my shepherd friend. I actually proved that in the months to follow when I simply decided that I would *make* time to be with him! Once again, my special friendship with Him is alive! I can truly say, it is *so good* to be walking with the shepherd again!

"I will give them a heart to know me, that I am the LORD. They will be my people, and I will be their God, for they will return to me with all their heart." —Jeremiah 24:7

CHAPTER 26

CLOSE TO THE
SHEPHERD'S HEART

The shepherd was watching over his flock while his sheep were grazing in the pasture. Most of the sheep were scattered across the field. Some of them were within ten feet of him. One little lamb was directly at his feet. I watched as the shepherd walked. Everywhere he went, the little lamb was always right by his side. Once in a while the shepherd would reach down and pet it. Whenever he did, the little lamb wagged his tail with joy.

I had to laugh at this sight. Most lambs are with a little group of other lambs, sleeping or playing in the fields. Others stick by their mothers. But not this little guy! He took great satisfaction in simply being close to the shepherd.

After observing this for a while, I walked out to my shepherd friend. I just had to ask him about that little lamb.

"Why does this little lamb follow you so closely wherever you go?" I asked him.

"His mother died," he responded. "I have to feed him with a bottle, so he likes to stay near me."

Throughout the years, I have seen many lambs that had to be bottle-fed. When I thought about it, I remembered that some of them ended up being quite close to the shepherd. Still, this one was different. He seemed so content just to be at the shepherd's feet. I watched a little longer. The shepherd picked him up. I could only imagine what it was like for that little lamb, having lost his mother, yet now happy to be in the shepherd's arms, so close to his heart.

Maybe you've experienced affliction in your life and you feel like that little lamb—so lost and wondering how you can go on. Life isn't always easy. Hardship comes—and sometimes tragedy, sorrow, and grief.

As I pondered this sweet friendship between the shepherd and the lamb, I realized that this little lamb's tragic loss is what actually brought him so close to the shepherd! It makes sense, though, because his nourishment now comes directly from the shepherd. He is fed from his own hand. He now has a special relationship with the shepherd and he *wants* to stay close to him!

In moments of difficulty or loss, we all have a choice. We can allow our trouble to destroy us and pull us away from God. We can become bitter and angry. Or we can allow our Good Shepherd to come and help us. We can determine in our hearts to stay at His feet and follow Him everywhere He goes, just like that little lamb. He will then come and feed us from His very own hand. In moments like those, we may find the most intimate of friendships as we feel His touch, hear His tender voice, and know Him like we would have never known Him before.

Today, if you choose to draw near to Jesus, our Good Shepherd, He will come and pick you up. You will be safe in His arms. You may even feel His heartbeat as He holds you close to His heart where there is peace, comfort, healing, strength, and love.

He tends his flock like a shepherd: He gathers the lambs in his arms and carries them close to his heart; he gently leads those that have young. —Isaiah 40:11

CHAPTER 27

IMPERFECT . . . BUT FORGIVEN!

Going out into the fields to walk with the shepherd has been one of my favorite past-times in Italy. These visits become even more special when I have an opportunity to help him! However, sometimes when I think I am helping, I'm actually causing him trouble!

Like the time I went to visit the shepherd and he tried to tell me to go around the flock, but instead, I went through it and chased after a few strays, not realizing that I was causing a great divide! I ended up causing him so much extra work that day!

Good intentions? Yes! But maybe if I'd consulted with the shepherd first I wouldn't have caused such problems . . . and gotten him so upset!

The amazing thing is that no matter how many times I have messed up or disappointed the shepherd over the years, he has always patiently forgiven me and allowed me to continue walking with him—and even helping him. I think *I* might have just given up on someone like me! But the shepherd appreciates my friendship and he sees my potential. He knows that even though I occasionally make mistakes, I am still a greater blessing to him than I am trouble. So as I keep coming back to him, he keeps forgiving me for my shortcomings while teaching me how to do things the right way. And as I continue to walk with him, my mistakes become fewer and fewer.

Probably one of my greatest weaknesses is simply the fact that I am *not* the shepherd! I wanted so badly for the sheep to let me near them so I could help the shepherd even more, but in the beginning, they were always afraid of me. At first, I was really frustrated by my limitations. The shepherd, however, didn't allow that to stop me from helping him. One day, he actually used my shortcomings to *his* advantage!

As the shepherd was watching over his flock, he heard the penetrating cry of a lamb that needed help. The shepherd looked up and saw the problem immediately. In the distance was a little lamb that had fallen into one of the small canals. He was frantically running back and forth, not knowing what to do. The shepherd wanted to help the lamb get out of the ditch, but the lamb was simply too distraught. It wouldn't stop running; it wouldn't come to the shepherd; and it wouldn't listen to him. I started to think that as long as that lamb kept running, the shepherd wouldn't be able to help it. I wondered what the shepherd would do.

Instead of losing his patience with that frantic little lamb, the shepherd came up with a plan. He placed himself at one end of the canal. Knowing that the lamb would be afraid of me, he asked me to go to the opposite end of the canal. At first, the lamb ran away from the shepherd, but when it saw me it immediately turned around and ran right to the shepherd where he could catch it and lift it out of the canal with his staff! That day the shepherd actually turned my weakness into something he could use!

This makes me think of times of suffering in my life when I have felt so weak. But Jesus, my Good Shepherd, used me—regardless of my personal weakness—to bring encouragement and great healing in others' lives! And that is how it is with our Good Shepherd!

There may also be other times when we want to do something great for God and then—BAMM!—the devil comes and reminds us of our imperfections or mistakes from our past. At that moment we may feel so unworthy to walk with Him, let alone be used by Him! It is incredible that not only has He forgiven us of our past mistakes, but He even allows us to continue helping Him—in spite of our shortcomings! He sees us, flaws and all. And somehow, He takes us and uses us—in spite of ourselves! Just like my shepherd friend did with me, He can turn our weakness into something He can use!

I think I can express it best by repeating some of my previous statements, changing a few key words: The amazing thing is that no matter how many times I have messed up or disappointed Jesus,—my Good Shepherd—over the years, He has always patiently forgiven me and allowed me to continue walking with Him—and even helping Him. I think *I* might have just given up on someone like me! But my Good Shepherd appreciates my friendship and He sees my potential. He knows that even though I occasionally make mistakes, I still end up being a greater blessing to Him than I am trouble. So as I keep coming back to Him, He keeps forgiving me for my shortcomings while teaching me how to do things the right way. And as I continue to walk with Him, my mistakes become less and less.

I may not be perfect, but I am forgiven! If God has forgiven me, I need to receive His forgiveness—and also forgive myself! From there, I can continue walking with Him . . . and I will be able to do *great* things for Him!

. . . being confident of this, that he who began a good work in you will carry it on to completion until the day of Christ Jesus. —Philippians 1:6

CHAPTER 28

THE STRAY LAMB

t's so wonderful waking up to the sound of bleating sheep. I leap to my feet and run to the window to see if I can catch a glimpse of the shepherd and his flock near our home.

This morning when I woke up, the shepherd was with his sheep on the other side of the field. I took the dog out for a walk. While we were walking, I heard the faintest high-pitched bleating of a little lost lamb on this side of the field. Even though it was so far away and his little bleating voice was barely noticeable, the shepherd heard him—from across the field! Immediately, he left his flock, went across the field, and called out to him. I looked out and saw a tiny little lamb. It heard the shepherd's voice and came running. Tears came to my eyes as my mind went to the Bible story Jesus told about the shepherd who leaves his flock to find a lost sheep and carries it back on his shoulders. As I watched, though, that wasn't how this story ended.

He called the lamb and it came. But then, it wandered off a bit. He called it, and it came back. Since the lamb kept straying, he took his staff to help guide it back to the rest of the flock. He even spanked it once with his staff. Still, the lamb kept going astray, so the shepherd picked it up by its legs and carried it back. I was somewhat surprised at his lack of gentleness. I wondered, why didn't he gently carry it on his shoulders?

My question was answered when he got back to his flock and loudly stated, "Sempre lui . . . sempre lui!" ("It's always him . . . it's always him!")

I pondered that for a while. Most of us have read the story that Jesus told about the sheep that wandered off and got lost. How many of us can relate to that sheep? We strayed from the path and found ourselves lost and away from our Good Shepherd. And then our loving Shepherd comes and finds us and lovingly takes us up in His arms and brings us back to Him and the rest of the flock.

What about the ones who just seem to keep going astray? Over and over again they wander away from the flock—away from the Good Shepherd. Sometimes all He needs to do is call their name. Other times He needs to guide them and even discipline them. But there is something worth noting: He *still* leaves the entire flock in search of that precious one that is missing—*even if* it is a little troublemaker!

Are you like that little stray sheep that keeps wandering away? If so, ask the Good Shepherd to give you a heart that desires to follow Him. If He has to discipline you, remember that it is for your own good. He disciplines those whom He loves.

Even though we may go astray over and over again, He still loves us. He *still* seeks us out.

May we always remember the wonderful love and extreme patience that our Good Shepherd has for us.

I will search for the lost and bring back the strays. I will bind up the injured and strengthen the weak.... —Ezekiel 34:16

CHAPTER 29

FEED MY SHEEP

One of my favorite things to do on Sunday evenings is to go out into the fields by our home and keep the shepherd company as he cares for his sheep. Sometimes I go alone; other times I take my husband or one of my daughters with me. I may stay only ten minutes, or I may linger an hour or two. Knowing that he is quite old, I try to make the most of every moment I have with my shepherd friend.

The shepherd and I were sitting on a broken stone wall on the outside of the field one Sunday evening. We weren't talking; we were just sitting there watching the sheep. As we sat there in silence, I realized it wasn't actually noiseless. As the sheep nibbled on the remains of the field that had been recently harvested, I could hear a constant *crunch, crunch, crunch*. Actually, the more I focused on it, the louder it got. All around me, all I could hear was the *CRUNCH, CRUNCH, CRUNCH* of 150 sheep and goats.

At that very moment, I felt like God was trying to tell me something. I listened deep within me, but all I could hear was *crunch, crunch, crunch*. I prayed for God to show me what lesson I might learn from sheep munching in a field, but nothing came.

After a while, I told the shepherd I needed to go. I shook his hand and ran back home.

It wasn't until a few days later that I understood what God had been trying to tell me. As I was walking the dog and looking through the fields, I heard God's still, small voice say to me, "Feed my sheep."

All of a sudden, visions flashed through my head—visions of the many experiences I have had with the shepherd and his sheep over these last few years. I saw visions of myself helping the shepherd with preemie lambs, seeking and saving lost sheep, and rescuing lambs out of ditches and thickets. I saw visions of the shepherd leading the sheep from field to field, caring for sick sheep, chasing off raging dogs, disciplining stray sheep, and making a path through a high field to bring the sheep to a new stream.

"Feed my sheep." Once again, I thought back to the sound of the sheep's constant munching. Sheep aren't like other animals that eat twice a day for ten minutes. The shepherd has to take them out of the pen and lead them to a field with fresh grass. They have to constantly munch for hours throughout the day before they can be satisfied. And the problem is, one field isn't enough. They normally go through at least four fields, go back to the pen for a few hours, and then go back through another three or four fields in the evening! That means the shepherd needs to be out with his flock for at least six hours a day—whether it is freezing cold or miserably hot outside! (And that's not even counting the duties back at the pen!) No, this is not a side job or a hobby. It takes a great deal of love, sacrifice, and commitment to be a shepherd. It can also be a very lonely job.

While the shepherd is out in the fields "feeding his sheep", anything can happen! From lost sheep, to stray sheep, to wounded sheep, to delivering sheep, to disobedient sheep, to dumb sheep, you simply never know what is going to happen in a day's work! But one thing is certain: the shepherd needs to be there for his sheep, watching over them constantly. Otherwise, they will find themselves in peril, they will go astray, or they will simply wander around aimlessly.

"Feed my sheep." Three little words. How many times have I read that sentence in the Bible—Jesus' command to Peter? Until I met my shepherd friend, it just seemed so simple. I always envisioned someone reaching out to the sheep with a bunch of hay in their hand, or a child at a petting zoo with some feed in a cone. But now, I was moved to tears as I realized that Jesus wasn't saying to Peter, "Go to the sheep every once in a while with a bunch of hay in your hand."

No, Jesus is our Good Shepherd. He knows all about shepherds and sheep. When He told Peter, "Feed my sheep," He was telling him, "I need you to lead my people—my sheep—to good spiritual food where they can grow and mature. You will need to watch over them, love them, teach them, care for them, protect them, rescue them, heal them, and carry them when they cannot walk on their own. I want you to go out and seek and save those who are lost." With those three words, Jesus was telling him, "I am calling you to give up everything and dedicate your *entire life* to feeding my sheep."

Jesus wasn't looking for a hireling. He was looking for a pastor with a true shepherd's heart. And that is what He is *still* looking for today.

"Feed my sheep."

Jesus asked him the third time, "Do you love me?" He said, "Lord, you know all things; you know that I love you." Jesus said, "Feed my sheep." —John 21:17

CHAPTER 30

THERE IS AN ENEMY!

A huge black dog came racing across a distant field. He spotted the flock of sheep and increased his speed.

I didn't even see him at first, but the shepherd saw him right away. "That dog is very dangerous for my sheep," he told me. I remembered that he had told me about him before.

At that moment, the dog burst into our field! He raced towards the flock! All of the sheep ran off in a mad stampede—all except for one little, weak lamb. The dog narrowed his hunt to the helpless lamb. With his mouth wide open he leaped towards it, ready for the kill. I closed my eyes. The last thing I wanted was to see a helpless little lamb getting killed by a dog. When the dog was just inches away from the lamb, the shepherd started running and yelling. *At the sound of his voice*, the ferocious dog ran away while the lamb fled to safety.

For several moments after that incident, I was stunned. It all happened so quickly. That ferocious dog came out of nowhere. I never saw it coming! But the shepherd was already aware of the potential dangers for his sheep. He was watching. He was listening. He was ready to act. It didn't matter that he was ninety years old! He *ran* to save his little lamb from the enemy!

So many times, I experience moments like these with the shepherd that, at the moment, seem so insignificant. I don't realize until later that God is trying to teach me a spiritual lesson. That's how it was with this incident.

I awoke in the night realizing that the big, black dog represents the devil. Whether he is coming at us like a roaring lion, a prowling wolf, or a ferocious dog, he has one purpose: to steal, kill and destroy. That is why we must always be on guard! He knows when to strike— when we are at our weakest. God's Word tells us to, "Be alert and of sober mind. Your enemy the devil prowls around like a roaring lion looking for someone to devour. Resist him, standing firm in the faith . . ." (1 Peter 5:8-9).

As we do our part in resisting the enemy and standing firm in the faith, we can be encouraged knowing that Jesus, our Good Shepherd, is always watching out for our souls. He sees the enemy when he is far off in the distance, even when we have no idea that he is there. In our time of need, He will come running to our rescue!

How wonderful it is to know that Jesus—our Good Shepherd—has all authority! *At the sound of His voice,* we are rescued from the enemy! *At the sound of His voice,* the enemy has to flee!

No matter what dangers we may face in life, we can know that our Good Shepherd is here to protect us. He is watching over us. We are safe in Him!

"The thief comes only to steal and kill and destroy; I have come that they may have life, and have it to the full. I am the good shepherd. The good shepherd lays down his life for the sheep." —John 10:10-11

CHAPTER 31

THE SHEPHERD'S KISS

have been blessed to have this friendship with the shepherd for seven years. He is now ninety-one years old—and he still passes by in the fields in front of our home! My friendship with him is so special that I have introduced each of my daughters to him. They are older now, and the oldest two are living back in the States.

When our daughter, Charity, came to visit us in Italy with her baby, one of the first things I wanted to do was to introduce little Ricky to my shepherd friend. Before I was actually able to take Ricky to meet him, I talked to Ricky about my shepherd friend and I read him the special photo book I made about my shepherd friend.

One day we heard that beautiful sound of the sheep bleating in the fields. I peeked out the window and saw that the shepherd and his sheep were very close by. We hurriedly threw on our coats and bundled up little Ricky. Then we ran outside before the shepherd and his flock went into the next field.

I had told the shepherd all about Charity and little Ricky in the previous months. Each time I saw him, he would ask me about them. I promised him I would take Ricky to meet him as soon as I could.

Today was finally the day! We walked down the path and eventually reached the shepherd. His eyes lit up when he saw that Ricky was with us. He was *so* happy he had finally come to meet him! He exclaimed, "Ciao bello!" (Hello beautiful one!) And then the shepherd did something that absolutely shocked us: he rushed over to Ricky, put his hands on his face, and greeted him with a big kiss—*right on his mouth!* Charity and I were speechless! No one had ever come to Ricky and just kissed him on the mouth like that! As the shepherd touched little Ricky's cheek and let him play with his staff, all Charity and I could think about was that unexpected kiss!

After we had talked for a little longer, we made our way back to the house. While we walked, I thought about the shepherd's kiss. While I would *never* recommend going to someone's baby and planting a kiss on their mouth, I began to understand that it was actually a beautiful demonstration of the great love he has for me and my family. He loves me and my daughters, so it makes perfect sense that he would love my daughter's son as well!

Bringing my family to meet the shepherd has reminded me of the process of introducing our children to the Lord. As parents, we should prepare our children—and our children's children—for that moment by talking to them about Jesus when they are very young. We should read them books about Him, especially the Bible, which tells them all about the Good Shepherd. As we pray and talk to Jesus about our children, we will find that He cares about them and loves them dearly. When we feel the moment is right, we must seize that opportunity to introduce them to Jesus, their Good Shepherd. He will be waiting anxiously for that day to finally arrive! When it does, He will rush to meet them saying, "Hello my beautiful one!" and then, He will surprise them with the Shepherd's kiss: an expression of love so great that comes when He forgives us of our sins and brings us to His heart.

"I have loved you with an everlasting love; I have drawn you with unfailing kindness." —Jeremiah 31:3

CHAPTER 32

FINISH TO THE END!

L ately, I've enjoyed going out to talk to the shepherd as the sun is setting. I usually just go out to talk to him when he is in the fields by our home, but one evening I found myself walking with the shepherd as the golden rays of the sun made a path that led him and his sheep back home.

That evening, I learned that, while it may be easy enough for the shepherd to get the flock to follow him as he leads them through the fields, it is much more challenging to get them on the narrow path that leads to home! Here we were, out in the field, so close to the sheep pen. If the sheep had looked up, they would have actually been able to see their home. A strange thing happened though. At the moment when it was time to go onto the narrow path that led them home, some of the sheep stopped listening to the shepherd and, instead of following him home like the rest of the sheep, they pulled away from the shepherd and the flock. Others saw the plush, green grass at a nearby house and veered off the path to eat that grass. Others yet veered off the path so far that they ran into a broken wire fence that actually captured them like a snare!

The shepherd directed the rest of the sheep onto a little bridge that takes them to the narrow gate that leads them home. Meanwhile, he called out to all of the stragglers. Some listened to his voice and found their way back to the right path. Of those that had gotten trapped in the wire fence, some were able to pull themselves free. Three of those sheep, though, really caught my attention. They were so ensnared that when they tried to respond to his voice, not only could they not reach him, but somehow, they got turned around—all three of them! It is a picture that—to this day—I cannot get out of my mind! They had been following the shepherd the whole time. They had been on the right path. They were *SO close to home*, and yet they got caught in a snare! No matter how they tried to get free, they simply couldn't. They were trapped. Turned in the wrong direction. Their legs were moving, but they were headed nowhere.

I just have to ask you . . . is that you today? Did you once follow Jesus, the Good Shepherd, only to find yourself off the path, caught in a snare, turned in the wrong direction, and headed nowhere? Jesus, your Good Shepherd, is calling out to you. Sure, you may find yourself so deep in sin that you can't get free on your own, but I can tell you that if you will call out to Him, He *will* come and save you! He will lead you back to the narrow path that leads you safely home.

What about those who have been following the Good Shepherd for many years? Maybe lately it's been kind of hard sticking to that narrow path. Just like those sheep, that green grass wasn't necessarily something bad, but it *was* a distraction. It made them take their eyes off the shepherd and it pulled them off the path.

How many people do you and I know who followed God faithfully for many years? They were so close to home—*they almost made it*—but then something came up. Something hurtful that was said or done to them that caused them to distance themselves from the flock, or a distraction like green grass that pulled them off the right path, or maybe a trap of sin, separating them from their Good Shepherd.

I want to encourage you today: DON'T GIVE UP! Keep your eyes on Jesus, your Good Shepherd! Follow Him all the way home! I pray that you would have a determination in your heart that, no matter what anyone else does, you would follow Him and remain true to the end. He's here to help you! It's going to be worth it! Press forward! Don't stop until you're safely home with Jesus, your Good Shepherd.

Finish to the end!

I have fought the good fight, I have finished the race, I have kept the faith. Now there is in store for me the crown of righteousness, which the Lord, the righteous Judge, will award to me on that day—and not only to me, but also to all who have longed for his appearing. —2 Timothy 4:7-8

CONCLUSION
HE KNOWS YOUR NAME

t has been almost ten years since I have walked with the shepherd. We got to visit him once when we went back to Italy for a trip, but sadly, I've never seen him again. I can't help but wonder how many years into his nineties he continued to shepherd his flock.

Before I returned to the States, I made the shepherd a beautiful book. It contained photos of us together, as well as some of the photos I took of his flock. I also let him know that I've been writing a book about all of our adventures together! He wasn't sure what to think about that, but I reassured him that God was using him and his sheep to teach many people about our Good Shepherd!

The last time I saw him, I said to him, "I want to thank you for what you have meant to me over the years."

He reached over to me and touched my hand. He said, "You have been a like a daughter to me." With that, he got choked up and wiped away some tears.

I looked into his eyes and saw love—the love of a father for his child. After all, that is what he had been for me during my time in Italy, far away from the rest of our family.

I am so very thankful for those beautiful seven years that I was able to walk alongside him, sit with him, talk with him, work with him, and learn from him.

When I think about him and his flock of sheep, I remember that it was nearly impossible for me to tell his sheep apart. There were a couple that I was able to distinguish over the years, but after some time, they all started to look the same again.

It wasn't that way for the shepherd, though. He knew each one of his sheep. I realized this for the first time when the shepherd singled out one of the 150 sheep in his flock. He said, "See that sheep? It's the one that was in the picture you took of us in front of the flock—the one that was standing by itself." Yes, I knew what photo he was talking about. One year for his birthday, I made him a framed photo of him and me. (It's the photo on the back of this book!) I was amazed that he had paid enough attention to the picture to know exactly which of his sheep were in it!

Even though my shepherd friend didn't give his sheep names, he most certainly knew each one of them individually. He knew all about them... and cared deeply for each and every one!

When one of his sheep had gone astray, he could tell you exactly which one it was. He could tell you which of his ewes was pregnant and approximately when they would be giving birth. He could tell you exactly how old each of his lambs was... just about to the day! That's quite amazing when you consider that he was ninety-one years old!

Jesus says a shepherd calls his own sheep by name. He goes on further to say, "I am the Good Shepherd; I know my sheep..." (John 10:14). If a shepherd knows his sheep and loves them that much, can you imagine how much more *Jesus* loves *you*? God also states that He is our Shepherd. Do you know what He says about you? He says that He has loved you with an everlasting love (Jeremiah 31:3) and that He will never leave you nor forsake you (Deuteronomy 31:8). He says He has a plan for your life—to prosper you—to give you hope and a future (Jeremiah 29:11)! He says that the very hairs of your head are all numbered (Luke 12:7); He says He knows you (Jeremiah 1:5) and even knows you by name (Exodus 33:17)!

If you are feeling alone, unimportant, or forgotten today, just know that Jesus, your Good Shepherd, has not forgotten about you! You are so special to Him! He knows all about you!

If you haven't done so yet, then maybe today is the day for you to surrender your life to Jesus, your Good Shepherd. He is also Jesus, the Lamb of God, who willingly gave His life for you and for me so that we might have forgiveness of sins and eternal life with Him.

If you will believe that Jesus is the Son of God, that He gave His life as a ransom for your sins, if you will repent of your sins and ask Him to forgive you, He will come and forgive you and cleanse you and adopt you into His family.

Jesus, the Good Shepherd, knows you by name . . . and today He is calling *you* to follow Him! Will you answer His call?

"My sheep listen to my voice; I know them, and they follow me. I give them eternal life, and they shall never perish; no one will snatch them out of my hand" —John 10:27-28

If you prayed and asked Jesus to forgive you of your sins, write down today's date below.

ABOUT THE AUTHOR

Angela and her husband, Rick were missionaries to Germany and Italy for 15 years. In 2014 God called Angela and her husband, Rick, back to the US to pastor a church in New Haven, Indiana. Around the same time, Angela felt God's leading to become a newborn photographer. She is the owner of Precious Baby Photography. (www.preciousbabyphotography.com) Angela's work has been recognized by millions of people around the world, as she shows the beauty and value of every human life. Her photography is especially known for her two projects: The Precious Baby Project and The After the Abortion Photography Series. (www.aftertheabortion.com)

Look for more books in the future, featuring Angela's stunning, faith-driven photography!

For speaking engagements, contact Angela at angelaforker@outlook.com.